John B. Cobb, Jr.

John B. Cobb Jr.

Is It
Too
Late
?

A Theology
of Ecology

Revised Edition

Environmental Ethics Books

Denton, Texas

Published by
ENVIRONMENTAL ETHICS BOOKS
1926 Chestnut Street, Suite 114
P.O. Box 13496
Denton, TX 76203-6496
SAN: 297-245X
Telephone: (817) 565-2727
Fax: (817) 565-4448

Editor: Eugene C. Hargrove

ISSN 0-9626807-3-7

This is a revised edition of the work published in 1972 by Bruce, a division of Benzinger, Bruce & Glencoe, Inc. Although small revisions have been made on almost every page, the book continues to reflect the views of the author from the time that it was originally published. The book concludes with an afterword by the author, written especially for this new edition, and a new bibliography of relevant environmental ethics literature covering the past two decades.

FIRST PRINTING 1994.

Printed in the United States
by E. O. Painter Printing Company
DeLeon Springs, Florida

Contents

Preface to the Revised Edition

Is It Too Late? A Theology of Ecology, originally published in 1972, was the first single-authored, book-length discussion of environmental ethics by a philosopher, appearing two years before John Passmore's *Man's Responsibility for Nature: Ecological Problems and Western Traditions,* which was actually an argument *against* environmental ethics. It was not until the late 1980s that a large number of comparable books were finally available—and those have proven to be less successful in addressing the needs and interests of concerned citizens, since they were written for academic audiences—primarily philosophers—not the general public. This book has been reprinted not only because it is a good non-technical introduction to the field, but also because it remains as relevant today as it was in 1972—and thus serves as an urgent warning that the issues Cobb discussed more than two decades ago *still* have not been adequately addressed!

—EUGENE C. HARGROVE

Preface to the Original Edition

Public awareness of the ecological crisis may increasingly dominate our cultural climate in the 1970s. Indeed, if it does not do so, there is little chance that measures needed for the survival of civilization will be taken in time. If the awareness does grow, it will seriously challenge us as Christians to rethink our faith.

Such rethinking will be neither comfortable nor easy. Our most fundamental picture of ourselves as human beings in relation to God and to a nonhuman environment will be at stake.

This book represents one Christian's response to this new questioning. I am led by my questioning to believe that the major forms of past Christianity are inadequate to our needs and must be superseded. But I have also concluded that it is fruitless to seek the vision we need in primitive or Eastern religions. Our task is instead to move forward to a new form of Christianity.

Obviously my idea of a new form of Christianity is only mine. It has no authority except its intrinsic merit. Some Christians will disagree that basic change is required. Others will disagree as to the appropriate direction of change. My hope is not to persuade all Christians to accept my conclusions, but to help to stimulate reconsideration of widespread attitudes and to encourage a debate that takes seriously the threat of doom under which we now live.

—JOHN B. COBB, JR.

What's the Problem?

The great question of the seventies is: shall we . . . begin to make reparations for
the damage we have done to our air, to our land and to our water?

—RICHARD M. NIXON[1]

Simple arithmetic yields astounding results. It shows that beginning with a
hundred dollars you only have to double your money ten times in order to have a
hundred thousand dollars. If you double it ten more times, you would have a
hundred million dollars. Since most of us could raise a hundred dollars, this is very
encouraging. It seems to make wealth more accessible than we ordinarily think.

But the same rate of growth applies in other areas where the results are
frightening. For example, if the world population continues to double about three
times a century, by 2300 it will have increased one thousand fold, and by 2633 it
will have increased one million fold. In 2300 there will be three and a half *trillion*
people, and in 2633 there will be 3,500,000,000,000,000. The latter figure is too
much for our imagination. The former is bad enough. In fact, one thing of which
we can be certain is that there really won't be three and a half trillion people in
2300. Can you imagine Japan with one hundred billion people, that is, thirty times
the present population of the whole planet? Or can you imagine China with eight
hundred billion, or even this country with two hundred billion? No, that is all quite
impossible. Something will happen to prevent it.

When driving across vast barren stretches of the American West, one might
recall that once great herds of buffalo found tall grass growing there. We know that
we slaughtered the buffalo, but we ask what has happened to the grass. Sometimes
the answer is that sheep were brought in and in a few years brambles took over.
Sometimes we learn that wells were drilled and the water table lowered. But there
were other, more favored lands to which people could move.

For some years those of us who live in Southern California have been complain-
ing about the smog. It stings the eyes, aggravates the sinuses, reduces the grape
harvest, and hides the beauty of the mountains from our view. We have been told
that it is the result of local problems of atmospheric inversion and that stricter
controls will take care of it.

From time to time an old swimming hole or a once fashionable beach is closed.
The sanitation department tells us it is no longer suitable for swimming. But we
can build fine new swimming pools and fill them with chemically purified water.
Streams and pools in which we once fished are now dead, but with our superior
transportation we can go higher into the mountains to catch fish supplied to those
lakes and streams by our public hatcheries.

In 1966 the East coast suffered a spectacular blackout because of an electrical
power failure. Less publicized failures are not infrequent occurrences. But more

generating plants can be built, and the electrical grid of the nation can be interconnected.

The last dodo died in 1689, and a hundred more species of birds have since vanished forever. But there are plenty of other birds. The California grizzly is extinct, but there are plenty of other bears. The giant Galápagos turtle will soon be gone from its native home, but the San Diego Zoo will preserve the species.

Both the United States and the Soviet Union have enough atomic weapons to destroy all humanity several times over. Their arsenals of chemical and bacteriological warfare are no less potent. But they exercise restraint.

One out of every four persons born today will carry through life the irreversible physical or psychological effects of malnutrition. Thousands starve every day. Protein deficiency stunts the normal development of intelligence. We are assured that agricultural technology will solve these problems.

Insect pests develop new strains capable of surviving chemical insecticides, while their natural enemies, the birds, are killed. We undertake to control the use of such insecticides while raising the official level of allowable contamination in milk and poultry.

For some time we have been more or less aware of one or more of these matters. We have felt some sadness, even a little anger, but we have accepted them as the price of progress. If the situation ever became really serious, we assure ourselves, our leaders would correct it.

It is only quite recently that we have begun to realize that all these problems are interconnected and cumulative. The attempt to solve one problem all too often worsens others. Furthermore, they are neither local nor temporary. The transformation of forests and grasslands into brambles and dustbowls has been going on for thousands of years. Ancient civilizations collapsed when they destroyed their agricultural base, but these were *local problems*. Now civilization is worldwide, and if our worldwide resources in soil are further depleted, there will be nowhere left to turn.

Smog may be an especially severe problem in the Los Angeles basin because of atmospheric inversion, but it is now a national and worldwide problem as well. The smog of Tokyo is breathed in California. It is not the air here and there, but the total planetary atmosphere that is being poisoned.

It is no longer just an occasional stream that has been turned into a sewer. Most of our major waterways are seriously polluted. Lake Erie is dead and Lake Michigan is fast dying. Even Lake Tahoe is affected! When Paul Ehrlich wrote a science fiction scenario entitled *The Year the Oceans Died,* projecting present trends, his date was not 2300 but 1979!

The problem of an adequate supply of electrical power is proving to be nationwide. Good sites for more dams are becoming scarce. The public is alerted to the risks of atomic power. The use of coal and oil pollutes the air and hastens the depletion of these resources.

Whereas species of birds and animals have become extinct throughout history, the rate is increasing rapidly. From A.D. 1 to 1800 one species of mammal was exterminated each 55 years. In this century the rate of extinction is one per year. Today the threat to their survival is wholesale. In some instances they are decimated by more efficient and ruthless methods of hunting. In others their ancient habitats are taken over. In still others their environment or their food is poisoned. Rachel Carson foresees a "silent spring" when birds will sing no more.

The United States and the Soviet Union may continue to exercise restraint in the employment of their ultimate weapons, but more and more countries are gaining possession of them. Even if these resist the temptation to use them, danger remains. The problem of storage and disposal of radioactive wastes has not been solved, and we dump outdated bacteriological weapons into the ocean on the untested assumption that the water will sufficiently dilute their virulence to prevent major damage.

Although we are making a little progress in controlling the use of DDT, we must remember that great quantities are already lying around in our soil and water, finding their way up the food chain to us, and being carried through the rivers to the continental shelves. We must watch helplessly as they do their work of damage both in our own bodies and in the minute marine life that is the basis for the food chain in the ocean. Virtually all of California's oceanic birdlife is already doomed. Meanwhile, our chemical industry continues to produce new products whose effects upon our environment are unknown. And while we are beginning to be more careful with our insecticides and weed poisons, the pressure of population on the food supply of the underdeveloped world greatly increases the demand for dangerous chemicals there.

At the moment, newly developed high yield grains are bringing about a "green revolution." Perhaps India will be able to feed its present population after all. This is cause for great rejoicing. But the risks, too, are great. The new strains of grain may prove subject to as yet unknown pests and diseases to which the native strains were resistant. The tragedy of the Irish in the last century points up the danger. There the whole national agriculture shifted to potatoes because of the quantity that could be grown. The population of the island multiplied. Then came the potato blight. Millions starved and other millions emigrated to save their lives. If the "green revolution" encourages the upward spiraling of India's already vast population, the result of a blight could be disastrous indeed! The present corn blight in this country reminds us that even our scientific and technological skills are sometimes impotent.

We are being made to realize that the problem of overpopulation is not one of the distant future; we cannot put it out of our minds with the assurance that something will happen before it becomes serious. It is a problem now. It is not a simple problem. Not all lands are crowded. In some cases the problem is more the rate of growth than the absolute population.

The problem of overpopulation is quite different in industrially advanced and in underdeveloped countries. In the latter, rapid increase of agricultural and industrial production is very difficult. Without outside aid a growth rate of two or three percent per year is difficult to sustain over long periods of time That rate of growth would be encouraging if it meant that living standards rose twenty to thirty percent per decade. But in most such countries the rate of growth of population equals that of production. Immense efforts are needed just to prevent further worsening of the already miserable quality of life. In countries where the population growth rate is very high, the battle is already being lost.

The industrial nations have a quite different problem. If their population growth rates were as large as those of many underdeveloped lands, they, too, would experience difficulties. If the population of the United States doubled in the next twenty years, we would not only have to replace all obsolete facilities, but also double the quantity of homes, factories, highways, schools, hospitals, post offices, food production, and so forth, just to keep up our present standards. This would involve as much production and construction in the next twenty years as we have managed in our total past history; and that would be no mean task even for us! But the population grows much more slowly in this and other industrialized lands. Raising the already comfortable standard of living is not difficult for us.

But it is just in these industrialized lands, and especially in the United States, that the other major problem of overpopulation arises—the problem of overconsumption. It has been estimated that the average American consumes from thirty to fifty times as much of the world's resources as the average Indian. Thus while the increasing population of India creates serious problems for the Indian people, their total impact on the resources of the planet is moderate. We, on the other hand, experience only minor and local ill effects from crowding. But it is our population, and not that of India, that threatens to pollute the skies and oceans and to make the whole world a far poorer place for our descendants.

Those who ridicule the idea that the United States should control its population when there is still much unpeopled land can argue that this country could support ten times its present population. They are right. Ten times our present population could live in this country on the standard of living now endured by the Indian peasant. But if we ask instead whether the world can afford a long continuance of even our present national level of consumption, the answer must be negative. If we wish to continue and pass on to our children anything approaching our present style of life, we are already overpopulated.

Furthermore, the underdeveloped world will not be content to wallow indefinitely in its misery while the industrial nations use up the remainder of the world's irreplaceable resources. A stable world order will require that the industrial nations cooperate with the others in their industrialization also, so that they may have hope of escaping their present treadmill. But it is simply not possible for even the existing world population to consume at the present American rate. There isn't that much to be consumed, and the total resources are declining, not increasing. If we are to set the norm for per capita consumption for the planet, we must learn to consume less as a nation.

I have been speaking of the exhaustible resources of our planet. It is widely recognized that fossil fuels are in limited supply, and it is obvious that if the average per capita consumption of petroleum in the world equaled that in the United States, the world supply would be used up in a few years. The same is true of many metals and minerals.

The story is similar with respect to timber and soil. Even now the forests of the world are being annually reduced. If the rate of consumption of timber products by all people averaged that in the United States, deforestation would be extremely rapid. And if we can conceive of increasing agricultural production around the world to the extent that all people ate as well as we Americans, the already disturbing rate of exhaustion of our topsoils would be accelerated.

Water and electricity are other significant elements in our consumption. Ours is a favored land, but already national rather than merely regional shortages threaten. Water can be reused several times over, but not indefinitely. In most parts of the world, even with the most careful management, the present population could not consume water as we do. There simply is not enough. Similarly, we have nearly exhausted the possibilities of hydroelectric power, and we generate much of our electricity from irreplaceable fossil fuels. There is no possibility of the present population of the world consuming electricity at our rate unless it is generated in other ways.

In making these statements I have largely ignored these other ways, and in them lies some hope. New sources of energy—atomic, for example—will be extensively employed to replace fossil fuels and waterpower. Chemistry will develop plastics to replace metals and minerals, substitutes for wood products will be found, and grains will be grown chemically without use of topsoil.

However, these technological solutions of the problems caused by the inevitable shortages are themselves extremely dangerous. We have already noted that radioactive wastes continue to pose a danger. In addition, the use of atomic energy generates immense quantities of heat that may seriously alter the temperature of the ocean. The proliferation of chemicals of unknown potency already endangers the living environment, and the rapid increase of dependence on the chemical industry is not compatible with the caution and restraint that are needed.

Furthermore, the replacement of our present dependence on fossil fuels, metals, and topsoil by sophisticated developments in physics and chemistry is an immense undertaking. The required scientific and technological competence is remote from the experience and potentiality of the majority of the world's peoples. The kinds of transformations of cultures that will be required for such changes cannot occur overnight. The world must have time to adjust. It has immense unfinished business dealing with the problems of the pollution it has already created and simply feeding its present population. We dare not accelerate the rate at which technological change will be required for physical survival.

We come finally to the specific warning of the ecologists. It is their province to show us how interrelated are all living things, both plants and animals, that jointly constitute what we call the Earth's "biosphere." The destruction of one species of life, however minor it may appear to us, can drastically alter the conditions of life for many other species. Similarly, the introduction of a new species into an area can upset the existing balance. We know too little about the consequences of these kinds of actions to plunge heedlessly on. Yet the rapid rate of change required to meet human demands leaves no time for the careful investigation that we need.

Fifty miles from Los Angeles and a mile above sea level the pines in the San Bernardino Mountains are dying from smog. An attempt is being made to replace them with smog resistant trees. This is a minor incident in the larger picture. But the death of these forests reminds us of the risk of thoughtless tampering with our environment. The survival of life itself may be at stake.

Is Ecology *the* Issue?

The ravages committed by man subvert the relation and destroy the balance which nature has established; . . . and she avenges herself upon the intruder by letting loose upon her defaced provinces her destructive energies. . . . When the forest is gone, the great reservoir of moisture stored up in its vegetable mold is evaporated. . . . The well-wooded and humid hills are turned to ridges of dry rock . . . and . . . the whole earth, unless rescued by human art from the physical degradation to which it tends, becomes an assemblage of bald mountains, of barren, turfless hills, and of swampy and malarious plains. There are parts of Asia Minor, of Northern Africa, of Greece, and even of Alpine Europe, where the operation of causes set in action by man has brought the face of the earth to a desolation almost as complete as that of the moon. . . . The earth is fast becoming an unfit home for its noblest inhabitant, and another era of equal human crime and human improvidence. . .would reduce it to such a condition of impoverished productiveness, of shattered surface, of climatic excess, as to threaten the depravation, barbarism, and perhaps even extinction of the species.

—GEORGE PERKINS MARSH[1]

These words, which were written over a hundred years ago by George Perkins Marsh, today ring with renewed urgency. America finally heeded the warning of Marsh and saved some of its great forests from irreversible destruction. But new means of destroying the environment, unforeseen by Marsh, threaten now to realize his worst fears. Irven Devore and Richard B. Lee write that "it is still an open question whether man will be able to survive the exceedingly complex and unstable conditions he has created for himself."[2] And David Lyle suggests that "the human race has, maybe, thirty-five years left."[3]

If the threat to survival is as serious as these scientists suggest, then suitable adjustment of our national priorities is the most urgent business of the seventies. The United States cannot solve the world's problems alone, but without American leadership the problems cannot be solved. We are the world's greatest consumers and polluters. We have done more than anyone else to release radiation and new chemicals into our environment. We have the resources to do something about the new problems. Other issues are urgent, but this one is imperative.

The danger in focusing attention on a single issue and raising it as one of supreme importance is that it might seem to detract from the importance of other issues. Those who are struggling for the rights of blacks, or browns, or reds, or students, or women; or for freedom in Brazil, or Greece, or the Soviet Union; or for the survival of Israel or justice for Arab refugees; or for peace in Southeast Asia, feel abandoned and cheated when their erstwhile allies move on to another cause while these battles are far from won.

An allegory will give perspective. Picture the world as a ship on a long voyage. The ship has first class and steerage accommodations. The crew directs its attention to the comforts of the first-class passengers, who have plenty of space, luxurious accommodations, and superabundant food of great delicacy and richness. In steerage men and women are crowded and uncomfortable. The food is tasteless and poorly cooked. Some suffer malnutrition. Contagious diseases break out, and medical help is inadequate. Tempers are high, and fights occur. First-class passengers occasionally look down on the steerage deck below with amusement and even with pity, but for the most part they prefer to forget the existence of these other passengers and to enjoy the gracious living for which they have paid. The fact that most of the steerage passengers are of other cultures and races makes this easier.

Many of the steerage passengers dream of someday transferring to first class and a few even succeed in doing so. But most resign themselves to the impossibility of such a move. They live in impotent envy, taking out their anger on each other. Finally, a few among them begin whispering that this is unnecessary. Why should they be crowded and poorly fed when there is so much space and food wasted on other decks? Why not share all the space and food equally? Many ridicule the idea as impossible, but others listen. Of these, some want to seize by force the space and food they need, while others propose appealing to the innate sense of fair play on the part of the first-class passengers. At first these win out, and a few changes result from their humble and modest requests. The food supply and medical attention are improved. The first-class passengers expect gratitude, but in fact the slight success only intensifies the demands for an equal share.

I will not detail the struggle as it grows bloodier and more bitter. The crew is called in by the first-class passengers to maintain order and guarantee their privileges—for which, after all, they have paid. And the crew obliges with all too little reluctance. The few first-class passengers who sympathize with those in steerage are increasingly ostracized. More important, many of the children of the first-class passengers believe in the cause of the steerage passengers and try to help them. Some of these also fall victim to the crew, while the parents generally think they have gotten what they deserve.

Several times during the struggle the news is heard that the boat has sprung a leak. A few members of the crew are dispatched to see about it. They report that it is not too large a leak yet, although it is growing. Most suppose that the captain will see to it and go on about their business and pleasure. But the captain is too busy trying to keep order, and the few who continue inquiring about the leak are ignored.

The untended leak becomes larger. Some of the ship's supplies are soaked in salt water and ruined. Even the boat's speed is slightly affected. New leaks begin to appear. Although life continues luxurious in first class, some notice that the ship lists a little. Some of the shipboard games are adversely affected. Shuffleboard is abandoned. More voices are raised about the urgency of action, but when the crew shoot some of the children, a new controversy breaks out which distracts attention.

The first-class passengers feel guilty about the killing of these children, but they cannot bring themselves to admit that they are in the wrong. They devote their energies to self-justification. The children are deeply hurt by this attitude on their parents' part. Until now they have felt that the ideals on which they have acted were those of their parents as well and that if only the parents saw the situation clearly they would aid the steerage passengers instead of using force against them. With far less confidence, the steerage passengers have shared this hope. But the willingness of the parents to kill their own children in order to maintain their privileges, and their subsequent justification of this act, is profoundly disillusioning. A few turn to unalloyed violence. Most relapse into angry but lethargic resignation.

The ship continues to list. Almost everyone recognizes it now. But in the aftermath of the intense emotions generated by the other conflicts, no one seems to care very much. Leaders vie with each other to announce their concern, but not one dares to speak realistically of the risk or of the vast cost of dealing with it. The people have no stomach for great sacrifices. Their idealism is spent.

This is where we are now. What happens next is still unsettled. We may continue to fragment into disgruntled minorities while frantic efforts on the part of our leaders to hold us together leave little energy to deal with the spreading leaks. Only when the water covers the lower decks will the passengers turn their attention, too late, to the problems of a sinking ship. With bitter mutual recriminations they will struggle for places in the inadequate life boats, while the sinking ship carries most to their death.

Another possibility is that the crew and first class passengers will wall off part of the ship in such a way that although the lower decks fill with water, the steerage passengers drown, and most of the supplies are lost, the ship can stay just barely afloat. In this way many of the first-class passengers can survive, although at a level of subsistence inferior even to that of the steerage passengers when the boat was intact.

A third possibility is that the ship's captain, as a person of wisdom and courage, will persuade all the passengers of the necessity of immediate massive action. Unnecessary supplies are then quickly thrown overboard, including many of the weapons used by the crew to control the steerage passengers. All able-bodied people join together in a massive effort to pump out the water and repair the leaks. In the process, the mutual antagonisms subside. New leadership patterns are established. All the passengers and the crew, as well, become a single community living frugally but harmoniously together.

Granted, only a miracle could realize this third possibility. Politicians would have to refrain from playing upon the mutual antagonisms of our polarized society and challenge us to extremely unpopular sacrifices. Masses of people would have to vote for and follow these politicians. Business and industry would have to adopt new criteria by which to measure achievements, and all of us who are dependent on the present system for our luxuries would have to accept a simpler style of life. Is all that really possible?

No one knows; but the unforeseen and the unexpected do occur. Indeed, the rise to consciousness of the ecology/population crisis itself illustrates the openness of the future, the occurrence of the unpredictable, the surprising fruition of forgotten seeds. I myself have been aware of its seriousness only since the summer of 1969. Yet even in that summer and fall one who was concerned felt like a voice crying in the wilderness. No popular national magazine had taken up the issue. The Church seemed silent. Politicians avoided the question. Only a few weary ecologists, nature lovers, and demographers kept up the apparently fruitless struggle to alert the nation before it was too late. The very word *ecology* was hardly known.

As late as February of 1970, Richard Register could point out the frightening analogy between the human reaction to ecological deterioration and a frog's reaction to the heating of its watery environment:

> There is an experiment well known among biologists in which a frog is placed in a large container of water and the temperature is slowly raised. The change is so gradual that the frog shows almost no sign of realizing what's happening. Then, almost peacefully, in temperatures approaching the boiling point, the frog dies—not with a bang, not with a whimper, but in pathetic ignorance.
>
> There is another experiment well known among the inhabitants of Los Angeles in which several million people are placed in a large flat basin bordered by an inversion layer at the desert fringes of that basin. Millions of cars and millions of tons of asphalt and cement are slowly added. The change is so gradual that the population shows almost no sign of realizing what's happening. . . .[4]

But Register's own article was a part of an upsurge of interest. The news media widely took up the new cause. New organizations arose and others gained fresh momentum and vitality. Politicians vied with each other in showing their concern. Ecologists and naturalists were in great demand. Ecology became a household word, and cars sprouted bumper stickers urging people to "control your local stork."

But there are already signs of waning interest! One hears flippant talk of someone having taken his eco-trip and being ready for something else. The events in Cambodia and at Kent State displaced ecological concerns on the college campuses.

At a superficial level this is inevitable. As soon as we move from description of the problem to proposals for action, we lose much of our confidence and conviction. No one really knows enough to answer our questions. Economists and ecologists often speak at cross-purposes, and we must listen to both. The issue is tied up with every other issue, and any step we take toward its solution has ramifications in other areas that are often bitter indeed. Many leftists are resentful about the emergence of this concern, since it distracts attention from their call for social revolution. Rightists regard it all as a Communist plot, since the problems cannot be solved without radical changes in our way of life.

It is profoundly unfortunate for our national health that our attention span is so limited. The problems of crime, race, and violence do not disappear when we turn to something else. Similarly, our environment will not recover from our assault upon it when we stop thinking about it.

For a while at least, our new attention to the environment will probably generate new interests. Now that we notice such matters, we find ever new indications of the seriousness of the situation. The recent discovery of mercury in our rivers is a case in point. The disappearance of various species of wildlife will not now go unheralded. We will be observant of our weather to see how it is being affected by our actions. The attention of the world focuses on the army as it dumps nerve gases into the ocean. If supersonic transports are as destructive as many expect, that destruction will not go unnoticed. There will be more public clamor against the commercialization of our remaining wilderness. Industry will have to consider more carefully how it disposes of its wastes.

But the question remains whether all this will lead only to a series of *ad hoc* measures designed to meet particular emergencies when public opinion demands it, or whether it will lead to careful planning and rethinking of our national life. The latter can occur only if a *new vision* of humanity and our place in relation to nature comes into being, a vision that would naturally express itself in a changed style of life.

Let the Engineers Handle It!

To a very large extent the problems now confronting us are technological. We must find means of disposing of our wastes that do not continue to poison land, sea, and air. We must find ways of generating energy that are less ecologically destructive. We must develop new modes of transportation. We must learn how to reuse much that we now throw away in ever mounting garbage heaps. We must develop new strains of rice and wheat to further the "green revolution" in the tropical world. New and simplified techniques of birth control must be found. These are all technological problems.

There is always the danger that this discussion of the philosophical and theological vision that is needed to deal with the ecological problems might seem to imply some disparagement of these technological tasks. It does not. But it does imply that the problems we face are not *merely* technological. We cannot simply continue to live and think as we have while assigning to the engineers the task of restoring the Earth.

An important illustration of the problem is the now oft-told story of the Aswan Dam in Egypt. Few countries suffer more acutely from the worldwide problem of overpopulation than does Egypt. For years it has depended on importing wheat for its survival. The modern, aggressive government under Nasser determined to deal with this situation. To produce more food required that more land be brought under cultivation. In Egypt this could be done only by irrigation. By constructing a dam not only could water be made available for irrigation, but also immense quantities of electrical energy could be generated to facilitate the industrialization of the nation. Forward-looking Egyptians carried through the project against all kinds of obstacles including the American government's withdrawal of support.

However, *Time* magazine reports:

> When an international team of ecologists studied the effects of the dam, they were shocked. For one thing, waterweeds are clogging the shoreline of Lake Nasser behind the dam. The weeds may well speed evaporation through transpiration to the point where the lake lacks enough water to drive the gigantic generators.
>
> The dam has also stopped the flow of silt down the Nile, which in the past offset the natural erosion of the land from the Nile delta. As a result, downstream erosion may wash away as much productive farm land as is opened up by new irrigation systems around Lake Nasser. Without the nutrient-rich silt reaching the Mediterranean, the Egyptian sardine catch declined from 18,000 tons in 1965 to 500 tons in 1968. As a final penalty, irrigation projects on the delta plain have allowed a moisture-loving snail to thrive. Since it carries schistosomiasis, most of the delta people have had that agonizing liver and intestinal disease.[1]

This story does not indict technology as such, and even in the instance cited, arguments may be given for the course of action followed. But it does indicate certain limitations of the technological attitude. We need to become clearer about these limitations.

In the first place, the function of technology is to manipulate, whereas what the nonhuman world often needs is to be left alone. Here it is the whole tenor of our culture that is called into question. Raw or untamed nature cries aloud in our tradition for humans to enter it to rule, to exploit, and to impose their own patterns of order. A beautiful wilderness area calls for "development." Wild animals are to be hunted, tamed, or put into zoos. An inaccessible area calls for roads and bridges. A meadow calls for cattle to graze it. A virgin forest calls for a sawmill and logging roads. When we do preserve some bits of our land from strictly economic exploitation, it is as scenery, as campsites, and for nature study. For these too, a certain amount of "development" is required.

Much of our manipulation of nature is highly desirable and even necessary. Without it, no properly human life would be possible. Also, where humans have seriously wounded the nonhuman world we cannot simply stand back and leave it to itself. Many species of wildlife would have died out altogether if they were not preserved in parks and zoos. The disappearance of forests would be accelerated if we did not fight forest fires. But this interventionist solution, to which we resort so readily, is sometimes more destructive than helpful in the long run. Often what the nonhuman world needs most is for us to leave it to itself. Given time and space it has immense powers of rejuvenation. But unless we can hold in check our technological mentality, unless we can guide our actions by a new consciousness or vision, we will not allow the nonhuman world the time and space it needs.

The vision we need involves the conviction that the worth of the nonhuman world is not only its usefulness to us but also its value in itself. With this vision we can develop the willingness to share our planet with other creatures. Then we will leave places here and there where the evolutionary processes that have produced these wonders, including ourselves, can continue unchecked. To these ends technology is irrelevant, and the technological attitude that has shaped us all is antithetical.

Technology and the technological attitude have a second limitation which is determined by their masters. They have developed chiefly in the service of economics and military power. Both of these have operated on the assumption that the nonhuman world has value only as it furthers pragmatic human ends. They have seen the environment as an essentially inexhaustible source of supplies to be possessed and processed. The whole engineering tradition is geared to the production of as much wealth or destructive power as possible, without regard to the question of long-range exhaustion of resources or pollution of the environment. This tradition will be transformed only if the total climate of opinion is transformed, and if society is reorganized to make its decisions in terms of long-range considerations of survival and well-being.

Thus far, hardly a beginning has been made toward such a change. Economic considerations remain dominant, and technology continues to serve these even where our very limited knowledge of the ecological need is quite sufficient to dictate changes. The government's vigorous support of the SST program is the most glaring current instance. The only justification for building the SST is that otherwise the United States will lose out to Britain, France, and the Soviet Union in the competition to supply planes to the world's airlines. According to our technological consciousness, bigger and faster airplanes constitute progress regardless of consequences and despite the fact that they are not needed. Since this technological consciousness will produce an economic demand for them, the administration affirmed that they should be produced, even though we already know they will be immensely destructive.

Fortunately, Congress refused to continue subsidizing this dangerous monster. It seems obvious that the sensible response to the threat of other nations' building and marketing SSTs would be to make clear that we will never allow them to fly over our country or to land at our airports. Since much of the projected use of these planes involves our airports, such a step alone would greatly discourage further development of the SST. In addition, some nations have already taken this step, and others would follow suit—especially if we led the way. We should seek through the United Nations to weld world opinion against these planes. Our national policy, if geared to saving the habitability of the planet instead of economic competition, would give priority to such matters.

This points to a third limitation of technology and the technological attitude. It embodies a false understanding of the relation of ends and means.

John Dewey used to stress that ends and means cannot be separated. Every end is a means to some further end. He was correct. But it is equally important to stress that every living thing is not only a means to be made use of by others but also an end in itself.

The technological attitude, however, makes a sharp distinction between ends and means. Engineers have ends assigned them. Their task is to discover and execute the most efficient means of achieving those ends. This leads to systematic blindness in three directions.

First, however sensitive they may be incidentally as human beings, the engineers as engineers do not regard the intrinsic value of the existing state of affairs with which their enterprise must interfere. They view the environment that they will alter as instrument or obstacle to their assigned purposes. Everything not specified for them as ends to be achieved is reduced to purely instrumental status.

Second, they do not attend to the incidental effects of tampering with the existing state of affairs. When they build a dam, they do not consider the long-term effects of changes in the aquatic life, even when these may affect the interests of fishermen and hunters. Their attention is concentrated on achieving the assigned goal.

Third, it is not for technologists to consider the wider implications and long-term consequences of achieving the goal. If the SST they are building proves in the end not even economically beneficial, that is of no concern to them. If it leaves vapor trails in the stratosphere, that is for other engineers to worry about later. Their task involves consideration of such matters only if relevant specifications are included from the first as part of their assigned end.

There would be nothing wrong with this if the technological attitude belonged only to the engineer. Somewhere there must be this concentration of attention on the efficient attainment of goals. But the technological attitude also affects those who set the goals. They aim at the winning of a war, or improvement in the balance of payments, or bringing more land under cultivation, or increasing the output of automobiles, with just the same isolation of ends from means that characterizes the engineer. Business and military life are compartmentalized. One is trained to consider particular aspects of the total situation as alone relevant and to appraise means for achieving desired ends simply in terms of those ends. Other consequences, either of the means employed or of the end achieved, are neglected.

What do people do today if they suffer from dizzy spells and do not know whether they are psychological or physical in origin? Perhaps you will say that they should first check the possibility of organic causes. Well and good. But they cannot simply go to "a doctor." There are doctors for skin, for feet, for hearts, for sinuses, for bones, for the sexual organs, and so forth. To what doctor then? If they knew what was causing the dizziness, the answer would be simple. But we are assuming they don't know. Who can tell them?

Perhaps we can advise them a little further. Dizziness might mean there was something wrong with the digestive tract, or with the ear, or with the circulatory system, or with the eyes. Of course there are other possibilities. Maybe they are simply overworked and would be cured by a rest. But how are they to find out? Must they diagnose themselves before they can decide which doctor to go to? Or can they perhaps still find a general practitioner or skilled diagnostician who can help them?

Many doctors know that all the parts of the body interact with each other and with the emotions as well. They know that this complex interaction of the parts with each other and with the whole is neglected when they treat only bits and pieces of the organism. Yet the pressures for specialization are immense, and with it comes, inevitably, the technological attitude.

Just as there are some doctors who resist the technological attitude and the accompanying specialization, so there are also some scientists who resist it. Of these, the most important for our present purposes are the ecologists. The ecologist insists that just as we do not have a multiplicity of parts of a body which are then only incidentally related to each other as a human being, so we do not have in the living world about us a multiplicity of individual entities which then have certain incidental relations with each other. When we study them in isolation from each other we do not understand them. The individual organism is constituted by its relations with other entities. Its dependence on these is not secondary but primary. Every change in one part of the ecological system affects the whole system.

The ecological attitude is the reverse of the technological one. It does not view the individual action in terms only of the end toward which it is directed but in terms of the whole network of effects that will actually follow from it. Each of these effects is in turn viewed as important both in itself and for the further effects that will follow from it. The ecological attitude does not put an end to manipulation of the environment, but whereas the technological attitude breeds confidence and ruthless haste, the ecological attitude breeds hesitation and caution. Whereas the technological attitude directs energies toward short-term goals, assured that new problems can be dealt with as they arise, the ecological attitude attends to complex and poorly understood consequences that may take years to work themselves out. The technological attitude assumes that with time all things are possible. It projects a future society of unlimited comfort, convenience, pleasure, and luxury, and unlimited extension through space and time. The ecological attitude suggests that the price of technological and economic progress may be too high, that there are limits, perhaps rather narrow ones, beyond which human beings cannot go, and that we must adjust to them soon or perish.

The Christian Responsibility

> Until recently, agriculture has been the chief occupation even in "advanced" societies, hence, any change in methods of tillage has much importance. Early plows, drawn by two oxen, did not normally turn the sod but merely scratched it. Thus, cross-plowing was needed and fields tended to be squarish. In the fairly light soils and semi-arid climates of the Near East and Mediterranean this worked well. But such a plow was inappropriate to the wet climate and often sticky soils of northern Europe. By the latter part of the seventh century after Christ, however, following obscure beginnings, certain northern peasants were using an entirely new kind of plow, equipped with a vertical knife to cut the line of the furrow, a horizontal share to slice under the sod, and a moldboard to turn it over. The friction of this plow with the soil was so great that it normally required not two but eight oxen. It attacked the land with such violence that cross-plowing was not needed, and fields tended to be shaped in long strips.
>
> In the days of the scratch-plow, fields were distributed generally in units capable of supporting a single family. Subsistence farming was the presupposition. But no peasant owned eight oxen; to use the new and more efficient plow, peasants pooled their oxen to form plow-teams, originally receiving (it would appear) plowed strips in proportion to their contribution. Thus, distribution of land was based no longer on the needs of a family but, rather, on the capacity of a power machine to till the earth. Man's relation to the soil was profoundly changed. Formerly man had been part of nature; now he was the exploiter of nature. Nowhere else in the world did farmers develop any analogous agricultural implement. Is it coincidence that modern technology, with its ruthlessness toward nature, has so largely been produced by descendants of these peasants of northern Europe?[1]

The author of these words, Lynn White, Jr. shows that technological developments in Western Europe did not await the rise of Western science or of a generally high level of culture. On the contrary, there were surprising advances even in the period sometimes known as the Dark Ages. By the year 1000 Western Europeans were applying water power not only to milling grain but to other industrial processes as well. By the early fourteenth century they had developed in two forms the weight-driven mechanical clock. When the Greek ecclesiastic, Bessarion, visited Italy in the mid-fifteenth century, he was amazed by the superiority of Western ships, arms, textiles, and glass, and especially by the waterwheels that sawed timber and pumped the bellows of blast furnaces. Later in the century it was technological supremacy that enabled even small Western European nations like Portugal to explore, conquer, and settle large parts of the globe.

These facts indicate the great importance of technological developments in shaping human society and human history. But in "The Historical Roots of Our Ecological Crisis" White is asking a different question. Why did these events occur in Western Europe when it was not the center of civilization? Obviously they cannot be attributed to superior intelligence or native genius. The question to be asked is why these peasants and artisans, even when the level of their general culture was primitive, turned their energies to technological developments in an unparalleled way.

The answer to this question can be found in their peculiar attitude, especially their view of the relation of humans and nature. This attitude was expressed in visual form in the early Middle Ages in pictures of humans receiving nature from God as their fiefdom. White notes that Frankish calendars "show men coercing the world around them—plowing, harvesting, chopping trees, and butchering pigs. Man and nature are two things, and man is master."[2]

The question as to the attitude that was conducive to the rise of technology is not raised simply out of curiosity about the past. That attitude is still present. The first Genesis account of creation, with its specific authorization of human dominance over the rest of the world, continued to be effectively operative in the West through the eighteenth century. Even when biblical authority became questionable in the nineteenth century, the vision of human lordship over the nonhuman world was not doubted. On the contrary, the rightful domination of humans was supposed to be self-evident and not dependent on the authority of revelation. Even the rise of evolutionary theory did little to give humans a sense of kinship with other animals. The Western unwillingness to leave things alone, to let the nonhuman world be, stems directly from this deep-seated Western common sense.

White's paper was addressed to a national assembly of scientists. His major thesis was that as long as the attitude and vision that have given rise to the ecological crisis continue unchanged, the problem is insoluble. Furthermore, the technology that has developed within the context of this attitude cannot be the instrument of its change. Since the attitude that is responsible for our difficulties is a religious or theological one, the change that is required must be at that level. Thus, White challenged the assumptions of those scientists who see all of our real problems as falling within the sphere of science and technology. He also challenged the complacency of Christians. Christianity is, at least in part, responsible for the technological attitude that has brought about our crisis and that still impedes effective action. Christian theologians must share in the rethinking of basic attitudes about humanity and its environment.

White shows the surprising extent of the independence of the development of technology from scientific advances. Even the industrial revolution occurred with little influence from any advanced science. The two were first effectively related in the chemical industries of the eighteenth century. The general application of scientific knowledge to technology began only in the middle of the nineteenth century.

Although technology alone has enabled human beings to change the face of nature, the present global crisis has emerged from the modern wedding of science and technology. Hence science shares with technology in responsibility for the threatening ecological disaster.

Earlier generations stressed the tension between science and Christian theology. Often their purpose was to discredit Christianity. They thought of science as a product of a reason free from religious faith or they attributed it to the Greek influence in the Renaissance. But more careful consideration from a less prejudiced point of view shows that the development of science in the West began in the high Middle Ages. It was continuous with the rest of the cultural activity and conviction of the time, and this was profoundly shaped by Christianity. The minds of the scientists were certainly free; but so were those of the philosophers and theologians of the period. A free mind is not one that is unaffected by its history or by the climate of opinion of its time.

Science can flourish when people believe that behind the apparent randomness or willfulness of phenomena there is an enduring order to be discovered. The understanding of reality as cosmos enabled the Greeks to make a brilliant start in the development of science, but on the whole, they preferred rational deductions to painstaking investigation of the facts. Islam made contributions—especially in medicine.

But it was the Western Christian view of nature as the creation of an intelligent will that provided the context and motivation for the sustained and patient effort, divorced from all consideration of practical results, that carried Western European science from its infancy in the Middle Ages to the amazing achievements of the seventeenth century. Because nature was seen as God's creation, one knew that it embodied rational and intelligible order. Furthermore, the discovery of *that* order was of supreme value since it led to knowledge of God himself.

Aspects of Christian belief have thus been responsible for Western European advances in both technology and science. Whereas that might have sounded like boasting a short time ago, in the light of our present problems it has the ring of confession. In this connection, there is still another basic aspect of Christian belief that has played its role in bringing history to its present pass. The Judeo-Christian tradition has deeply implanted in the Western psyche the idea that every human individual is of absolute value. Of course, the actions of nations and individuals have repeatedly violated this principle. But that is not the point. The positive effect of the principle on national and individual action has been enormous. Vast efforts have been expended to keep alive human beings whether or not they are able to make a contribution to society. A large portion of scientific and technological advancement has been successfully directed toward the conquest of disease and the prolongation of life. The Westernization of the globe in this respect has played a major role in the vast increase in worldwide population in the last fifty years.

When this high appraisal of the value of the human individual is brought together, as it has been in Western Christianity, with the view that humans are called to dominate the nonhuman world, this world is still further reduced in value. Indeed, it has been denied any value in itself. Its value lies entirely in its usefulness to people. Only human beings have intrinsic worth. The value of the nonhuman world is purely instrumental.

These convictions have provided the overarching context for our technological dealing with the world. If they remain intact and continue to govern our use of technology, what consequences can we expect to follow? We might continue basically on the course we have followed thus far. We would then view the progressive breakdown of the ecological cycle as reason for accelerating our scientific investigations and technological progress. We have already moved far toward substituting an artificial environment for a natural one. If the planet cannot support both a vastly increased human population and high grades of nonhuman life, we would destroy the latter and learn to produce what we need artificially out of the inanimate resources of the planet or from the lowest grades of the animate. We would build vast cities under plastic domes surrounded by poisoned air, polluted water, rock, and dust. The nonhuman world would then indeed be little more than the mere "it" we have treated it as being.

Whether such a direction is even possible no one today really knows. Could science and technology sustain a larger population in this wholly artificial context than can be sustained by achieving ecological balance? Would it turn out that human beings have either biological or psychological needs that could not be met in this way? Would the changes in temperature, sea level, and radiation be so drastic that survival would be impossible despite scientific progress?

Even if this direction were possible, one may question the wisdom of those who would choose it. The attempt to evaluate a type of life profoundly different from any we have known is fraught with hazards. It is difficult to think of existence in such a world as even human, much less happy. The absolutization of human life at the total expense of nonhuman life seems to lead to a mode of being in which human existence itself would be nonhuman in quality.

In any case, we know that we do not presently have the science or technology to sustain human life on a dead planet. If we press on in this direction, most of the world's present population and its immediate offspring must be sacrificed. Perhaps a hundred or a thousand years from now humanity will be faced with a serious choice between increasing population and retaining a living environment, but today the living context remains essential to the maintenance of human life as well.

On this ground alone, then, one who holds the traditional evaluation of humanity and nature should agree to devote vast energies to nursing the environment back to health while stabilizing population. At present, nonhuman life is necessary to human existence and, therefore, of immeasurable instrumental value.

Without a recognition that humanity *needs* a healthy environment, there is no possibility of making the changes required to heal the nonhuman world. Self-interest is a necessary motivation, but it is not sufficient. This insufficiency was illustrated in the conservation movement. As a leader in that movement, Aldo Leopold noted its actual impact. In the thirties farmers were called on to adopt new approaches in the name of enlightened self-interest. They responded well. But in the absence of disinterested concern for their land, they adopted only those practices such as contour farming that had short-run economic advantages. In *A Sand County Almanac* Leopold wrote in 1949 that "the education actually in progress makes no mention of obligations to land over and above those dictated by self-interest. The net result is that we have more education but less soil, fewer healthy woods, and as many floods as in 1937."[3]

Non-Western Views of Nature

In *The Making of a Counter Culture* Theodore Roszak gives voice to the horror with which many sensitive persons view our dominant inherited attitude toward nature. "Whatever our degree of intellectual sophistication," he writes, "we shall as a culture continue to deal with our natural environment as lovingly, as reverently as a butcher deals with the carcass of a dead beast."[1] To throw into relief the harsh brutality of our dominant practice, he quotes a Wintu Indian woman describing the contrasting relation of her shamanistic culture and that of white people to a common environment.

> The white people never cared for the land or deer or bear. When we Indians kill meat, we eat it all up. When we dig roots, we make little holes. . . . We shake down acorns and pinenuts. We don't chop down trees. We only use dead wood. But the white people plow up the ground, pull up the trees, kill everything. The tree says, "Don't. I am sore. Don't hurt me." But they chop it down and chop it up. The spirit of the land hates them. . . . The Indians never hurt anything, but the white people destroy all. They blast rocks and scatter them on the ground. The rock says, "Don't! You are hurting me." But the white people pay no attention. When the Indians use rocks, they take little round ones for their cooking. . . . How can the spirit of the earth like the white man?. . . Everywhere the white man has touched it, it is sore.[2]

We can immediately sense the ecological significance of such a passage. Here is a people who seek in every possible way not to interfere with their environment. Their motivation is not the human-centered one we have been considering. Instead, it includes a concern for trees and rocks that is like that for other human beings. Self-interest plays a role, since the Indians desire that the spirit of the earth like them. But pragmatic estimates of consequences to themselves are not primary. The Indians have observed the white people getting away with it for generations. What is primary for them is a vision of reality in which they and their world belong together in a unity.

Stewart Udall in *The Quiet Crisis* writes:

> The most common trait of all primitive peoples is a reverence for the live-giving earth, and the native American shared this elemental ethic: the land was alive to his loving touch, and he, its son, was brother to all creatures. His feelings were made visible in medicine bundles and dance rhythms for rain, and all of his religious rites and land attitudes savored the inseparable world of nature and God, the Master of Life. During the long Indian tenure the land remained undefiled save for scars no deeper than the scratches of cornfield clearings or the farming canals of the Hobokams on the Arizona desert.[3]

Primitive humans hunt animals for food. But they sense in the destruction of animal life a violation of the animal that must somehow be atoned. They often ask the pardon of their animal victims when it is their painful duty to kill. The primitive Kafirs hunted the elephant. But when they had killed it, they assured it they had not done so on purpose.

If human beings had remained primitive in spirit our ecological crisis would not have arisen. Primitive life was in fundamental balance and harmony with the animate and inanimate world around it. This harmony was not mere chance or simply the result of the lack of means for mastering and destroying the environment. Mastery and destruction were not sought. The aim was rather to leave the environment alone as much as possible, to interfere with it only as necessary for the well-being of the tribe, and to surround these interferences with ceremonies designed to express their exceptional and unfortunate character.

The difference between primitive people and ourselves is not to be interpreted as a relative lack of intelligence. Their languages are very complex and express many distinctions we do not ordinarily perceive. They have an awareness of distinctive features of the world which escape our attention. But as Ernst Cassirer notes in *An Essay on Man,*

> . . . in his conception of nature and life all these differences are obliterated by a stronger feeling: the deep conviction of a fundamental and indelible solidarity of life that bridges over the multiplicity and variety of its single forms. He does not ascribe to himself a unique and privileged place in the scale of nature. The consanguinity of all forms of life seems to be a general presupposition of mythical thought.[4]

Thus the difference between primitives and ourselves is a difference in mode of consciousness. We experience our worlds differently. Whereas we objectify our world, they participate in theirs. We seek and attain dominance. They seek and attain balance.

Does this mean that the new consciousness that we need is the consciousness already realized in the primitive? Roszak does not go quite that far. He knows that there can be no simple return to the past. Yet he does see in the primitive shaman a model for the consciousness we need. Is he right?

At one level he seems to be. We would be enriched if we could recover the immediacy and intimacy of the primitive's relation to plants and animals. Primitive people's respect for the world and their effort to live in harmony with it could guide our responses to the ecological crisis. This spirit of kinship and unity would check our spirit of conquest and indifference.

But Roszak goes much too far in idealizing the primitive vision. Although there was warmth and joy in the primitive's intimacy with nature, there was also terror and guilt. As Erich Neumann aptly describes it:

> Exposed to the dark forces of the world and the unconscious, early man's feeling is necessarily one of constant endangerment. Life in the psychic cosmos of the primitive is a life full of danger and uncertainty; and the daemonism of the external

world, with its sickness and death, famines and floods, droughts and earthquakes, is heightened beyond measure when contaminated with what we call the inner world.[5]

We must realize also that the failure to distinguish sharply between human beings and nonhuman entities not only caused primitives to respect the latter more but also to respect the former less. Human life was comparatively cheap. In overcoming our alienation from nature, a return to the primitive consciousness would involve also the loss of our hard won sense of human dignity and worth.

Further, the vision of primitives did not prevent them from adopting ecologically destructive practices. On occasion Indians drove herds of buffalo over cliffs and then ate only their tongues. With the advent of the horse, they increased their rate of killing the buffalo so much that some scholars believe they would have exterminated the herds even without the aid of whites.

Finally, there are practical considerations. If we were so foolish as to attempt a return to a primitive world the vast majority of us would have to die. The present population is supported by aggressively modifying and utilizing the environment in a way alien to the primitive spirit. With the bear and the buffalo, and the wild turkey and the beaver almost gone, and the fish in many rivers killed by pollution, the American land could not support even the pre-Columbian Indian population if we lived as they did—and that was a tiny population in comparison with ours.

Of course there is no possibility of return to the past, however idyllic it may appear, but if we could and did return, we would be appalled by the actuality of what we found. As a result, if the choice were between moving forward toward a wholly artificial environment, with technology almost wholly replacing the natural environment, and returning to a primitive existence, we would be forced to choose the former, however horrible it might be.

However, the choice may not need to be between a primitive existence and a fully technologized one. In the East, high civilizations have been built in conjunction with sophisticated views of reality that nevertheless share with the primitive the sense of balance and harmony with nature.

In Israel human beings established themselves as such by distinguishing themselves from the rest of nature and setting themselves apart from it. To some extent this was true also of Confucianism in China. But the deeper Chinese vision did not accept this divorce of humanity from nature. In Western painting the nonhuman world sometimes appears as background or context for human presence or action, sometimes as artifact, or as game, or as still life, and occasionally as somewhat anthropomorphized or sentimentalized wilderness from which human beings are absent. A human being can hardly appear in Western art without dominating the scene. In Chinese landscape painting, on the other hand, people are presented as part of nature, harmoniously related to the whole, but no more than one part among others.

The influential concept of *féng-shui* involves the adaptation of human buildings and roads to the cosmic spirit or breath. This leads to construction that blends into the landscape rather than dominating it. Natural curves are preferred to straight lines.

This Chinese vision is in greater continuity with the primitive vision than is the humanism of Israel or Confucius; but it is far from primitive. Especially in its Taoist form, it represents a position of high sophistication and great appeal to the cultivated Western mind. In Taoism the goal is the recovery or renewal of the primordial harmony of heaven and earth. This is not achieved by intervention in the world, either human or nonhuman, but by *in*action. As George Foot Moore notes: "Not to bring the universe, by activities of any kind, into harmony with man's desires, but by pure passivity to be in harmony with the universe, is the way to be blessed."[6]

To prize inaction does not mean literally to give up all physical movement. What it does mean is to give up interference in the course of society or nature. Well-intentioned social reforms are just as objectionable in this respect as are sinister manipulations for selfish ends. People should avoid intervention in the natural simplicities rather than try to shape events to fit their purposes.

The ideal quality of life expresses itself in gentleness, humility, and frugality. But these are not virtues to be strenuously cultivated. Rather they are the consequences that follow the abandonment of all desire that things be other than they are. Contentment with life as it is allows the individual's existence to blend with encompassing *Tao*—that is, the original and fundamental and unchanging Way.

> The Great Tao is all pervasive; it may be seen on the right and on the left.
> All things depend on it, and are produced; it denies itself to none.
> It achieves its works of merit, but has no name or reputation. With tenderness it nourishes all things, yet claims no lordship over them.
> It is ever passionless, and may be named among the smallest things.
> All things submit to it, yet it claims no lordship over them, it may be called great.
> Thus the Sage to the end of his life never exalts himself; and thus he is able to achieve great things.[7]

If the Taoist attitude had dominated human history, technology and science would not have developed. People would not have been driven to preserve and extend human life. The natural cycles of abundance and famine would have continued to be accompanied by the increase and decrease of population. People would have accepted these cyclical changes without resentment or ambition. There would be no ecological crisis.

At first glance Taoism seems to have the advantages of the primitive consciousness without its liabilities. Taoists have no terror of either the external or the internal world. They are also free from guilt. They are not, like primitives, undiscriminating in their reactions or lacking in freedom. They know human life as human and value it as such. Moreover, the Taoist vision seems to have been compatible with the long survival of a great nation with advanced technology.

Nevertheless, before we suppose that in Taoism we have the consciousness that is needed, we should note the historical facts. Taoism did not control actual Chinese practice in relation to the natural environment. The Chinese deforested vast areas of their land as thoroughly as did any other people despite some awareness of the consequences. When the aesthetic and passive preferences of the Chinese conflicted with their economic needs, the latter were generally determinative. Although some Taoists refused to employ technological advances, Chinese society as a whole prized them. The Taoist passivity in relation to social and political processes restrained Taoists from preventing the ecologically destructive practices of others.

If Chinese deforestation and other ecologically destructive practices were simply typical of all populous civilizations, it would count but little as an objection to our adoption of Taoism today. But we find that in much of Western Europe there has been a sustained and quite successful effort to save large sections of forests. It is *Communist* China, which shares the Western passion for mastery and use, that is engaged in widespread efforts at reforestation. In this respect the attitude of dominating nature has worked better than the more quiescent Taoist one. Domination can mean careful and sustained management rather than ruthless destruction. Even if destruction represents lack of foresight and planning rather than the desire to master and control, it is still destruction, and all the disastrous consequences follow. If we adopted the Taoist attitude today, the results would more likely be continued deterioration of our resources rather than effective conservation.

Here, too, Marsh's vision was prophetic. Humankind cannot now leave a wounded nature to its fate. Instead, it must

> . . . become a co-worker with nature in the reconstruction of the damaged fabric which the negligence and wantonness of former lodgers has rendered untenable. [It] must aid her in reclothing the mountain slopes with forests and vegetable mould, thereby restoring the fountains which she provided to water them; in checking the devastating fury of torrents, and bringing back the surface drainage to its primitive narrow channels.[8]

What we need, then, are active efforts to save our environment based on adequate scientific information and technological skill. The vision we require is one that would encourage and guide long-range planning and vigorous efforts. To this end, neither the primitive nor the Taoist vision would be effective.

A New Christianity

If the continuation of our present direction leads to horror, if the return to a primitive consciousness is impossible, and if we cannot afford the quiescence and poise of Taoism when so many changes are needed, where shall we turn? The answer is that rather than seek to recover something that is lost or to leap into an alien tradition we need to go forward in the transformation of the tradition in which we now stand. To do so, we should seek within our tradition those submerged elements whose new prominence would give us the vision or consciousness we need.

In Christian history there are two figures who stand out for their participation in the consciousness we need: Francis of Assisi and Albert Schweitzer. Francis' respect for his brother the wolf and his sisters the birds was not less real than that of the primitive, but it differed profoundly. He did not abandon Western rationality; he went beyond it. He knew none of the guilt that pervades the lives of primitives. Although his life was hardly less precarious than theirs, he did not share their terror.

Francis may be too remote from our skeptical day to be a persuasive teacher. Probably his practice was too extreme to serve as an effective model of the new Christianity. Few of us will want to preach to birds. But this objection does not apply to Schweitzer. He lived among us very much as a citizen of our time. In turning his back upon the comforts and advantages of a successful life in Europe he was not rejecting the achievements of European culture. He continued throughout his life to contribute to the philosophy and theology of Europe as well as to its music. It was *modern* medicine he went to Africa to practice. Further, Schweitzer was free from sentimentality. He was not credulous. Few Western humanists find his ideas difficult to understand.

What Western humanists and Christians do find difficult is to adopt Schweitzer's self-giving devotion to the service of human need and his vision of all life as worthy of reverence. The former stands squarely in the tradition of Christian devotion. The latter transcends or extends it.

In Schweitzer's words:

> The ethics of reverence for life is the ethics of Jesus, philosophically expressed, made cosmic in scope, and conceived as intellectually necessary.
>
> The great error of earlier ethics is that it concerned itself only with the relations of man to man. The real question is, however, one concerning man's relations to the world and to all life which comes within his reach. A man is ethical only when life, as such, is holy to him, that is, the lives of plants and animals as well as the lives of men. Moreover, he is ethical also only when he extends help to all life that is in need of it. Only the universal ethics of the ever-expanding sense of responsibility for all life can be grounded in thought. The ethics of the relation of man to man is not something unto itself. It is only a particular application of universal ethics.[1]

Thus it is clear that the extension of concern to all living things is a movement neither backward nor away from our Christian heritage. It is a movement forward in the inner transformation and further development of this peculiar tradition.

The tradition began in ancient Israel. Israel grew out of the primitive immersion in nature by affirming human primacy within nature. Since the God she worshipped was the creator of all nature, neither nature as a whole nor any portion of it could be viewed as sacred. Israel denied the existence of the Wintu Indian's spirit of the earth. She accepted all of creation as given to humanity for its well-being.

Nevertheless, the natural environment was not reduced simply to means. In that first chapter of Genesis, so fateful for the course of human events, God perceives that the nonhuman world is good. God sees this quite without reference to human beings. Its goodness is intrinsic. It shares with humanity the status of creature-hood. It participates in witnessing to God's greatness. Thus when human beings are freed to govern the world, the world they govern is not thereby reduced to mere means to their end.

Christianity introduces a more radical self-transcendence. The intensification of freedom and individuality that is involved separates humanity from the nonhuman environment even more drastically than did the personal existence of the Jew. At the same time, the contrast between what is and what ought to be, already vividly developed in Jewish apocalypticism, is intensified. Original sin and its cosmic consequences are keenly felt. People are turned toward God and one another, and their natural environment almost loses significance. What emerges is an extreme humanism, a strong sense of human internality, infinitely important selfhood, and radical transcendence over the nonhuman world. The profoundly self-conscious individual could escape the misery of self-preoccupation only by authentic love of others.

Not only is love essential to the Christian in a new way, but also the quality of this love is new. Whereas for the Jew love of neighbor meant justice and righteousness in the treatment of neighbors, for the Christian love of neighbors means an actual concern for them as fellow human beings. Such concern should express itself in just and righteous treatment, but it is not motivated by the desire to be righteous. In that sense it is the motiveless motive of Christian action. It is directly connected with the absolute valuation of every individual life, which we have recognized as the foundation of our traditional ideals.

This high valuation of human life in its individuality and particularity is susceptible to two developments in relation to the nonhuman world. First, the focus upon what is distinctively human and inward tends to widen the gulf between humanity and other living things. This can lead, and has indeed led, to the absolutization of this gulf that has dominated modern Western ideals. The second possible development is that the concern for others, now directed toward fellow human beings, can be extended to nonhuman life as well. This extension of love has been a subdominant element in the modern West.

In Francis of Assisi and Albert Schweitzer, there is a disinterested love of nature quite unlike the primitive attitude and going beyond the Old Testament recognition of the goodness of all creation. This love of nature involves no disparagement of humanity, for we are the apex and summation of nature. It need not prevent us from continuing our scientific investigations of nature. Indeed, it can provide such inquiry with a deeper motivation, a level of motivation that has been lacking since the acids of modernity destroyed the vision of divinely imposed order. It need not reject technological manipulation of the nonhuman world where that is needed for the sake of a richer human life. But it would prevent ruthless indifference to the consequences of our actions for the living environment. Every human action must be measured in terms both of its consequences for us and of its consequences for other living things. That we are of vastly greater worth than any other creature does not reduce the value of the others to nothing.

But Westerners have translated this relative superiority into a radical disjunction. Especially since Kant, thinkers have feared that to treat humanity as part of nature would turn us into mere objects. Such objects would have no intrinsic value or at best no greater value than dogs and cows. But such a fear is ill-founded. By distinguishing within nature the human and the nonhuman, we can continue to recognize the superior value of human beings without disparaging or denying the intrinsic value of other living things.

The extension of Christian love beyond human beings to other living things, which is justified and demanded by this vision, is a continuation and development of our biblical Christian heritage rather than its repudiation. Nevertheless, the Christianity that will emerge is significantly new.

Fuller discussion of the *new* Christianity will be found in the last three chapters of the book. Here, just one topic will be considered—the question of the sacredness or absolute value of *human* life. That human life is an absolute has been the fundamental dogma of the modern West, shared by Christians and non-Christian humanists alike.

The deep-seated sense of something sacred or absolute persists in our highly secularized age, but it is often unrecognized. To bring it to consciousness, let us consider first our attitude toward incest. We can give good pragmatic arguments against sexual intercourse between a son and his mother. Its practice is incompatible with wholesome family life, and there seem to be some genetic disadvantages for the offspring of such unions. But the feelings many people have about incest are disproportionate to its harmfulness. To them it seems absolutely wrong; it would still be wrong even if psychologists, sociologists, and geneticists provided evidence that its widespread practice would be beneficial.

The sense of sacredness or absoluteness attaches not only to ethical principles but more fundamentally to entities. Some hold their country sacred. This attitude is expressed in the common meaning of the saying "My country right or wrong" or, more recently, "America, love it or leave it." These sayings imply that commitment or devotion to one's country does not depend on its contribution to the good of humanity in general or even to its own citizens. It is an absolute. Americans who thus view their country as a sacred object judge other nations and individual Americans according to their contributions to the interests of the United States, but they do not judge the United States by any higher norm.

Humanists condemn this idolatrous attitude toward a nation-state. They affirm patriotism, but one's higher loyalty should be to the good of humankind generally. It is in this object that humanists find *their* absolute. To the question of why it is appropriate to serve humanity, there is no answer. Either one recognizes the absolute worth of human beings, individually and collectively, or one does not. The humanist refuses to judge individuals in terms of their contribution to society. Whether or not individuals contribute to the wider community, they are of absolute value in themselves. That means human life is sacred.

To view human life as sacred is to believe that its value is beyond calculation, that it is incommensurate with all other values, and that it should be treated only as an end and never as a means. The inculcation of this view, both of oneself and of one's neighbors, has been at the heart of Western moral teaching. Modern ethics, in both its utilitarian and its Kantian forms, takes *human* good as its unquestioned context.

Of course, we have been far from consistent in our affirmation of the sacredness of human personality. We have made official exceptions in the cases of capital punishment and just war. Clearly we have, in fact, calculated about the value of one life in comparison with others. But in spite of these exceptions, the sense of absoluteness with respect to the value of human life has controlled large areas of our attitude and practice.

The influence of this doctrine has been widely beneficial, but we are now recognizing that it has harmful consequences as well. Only one thing can be absolute. If human values are absolute, then other animals have value *only* as they serve human ends. It logically follows that any amount of suffering may be inflicted on animals if the result is some enhancement, even a slight one, of human enjoyment. And practice follows theory: We torture horses, for example, by tightening a strap around their kidneys and intestines so that we can enjoy "bucking broncos" at our rodeos, or by "soring" their front feet we force them at the price of agony to walk in ways we find entertaining in our horse shows.

Even more seriously, we have seen, the lack of concern for the nonhuman world continues to lead to actions that threaten human survival as well. Hence, in order to foster this wider concern, we must challenge and alter the basic principle of humanism itself. The change would be modest if we could simply extend to other forms of life the sacredness attributed to human life. But that is not possible. We can forbid cannibalism, but we cannot forbid the eating of other living things. Even if we insisted on vegetarianism, declaring only animal life sacred, we would still have to kill some animals for the sake of others, or else let all the carnivores in our zoos starve. Schweitzer was forced to kill fish to save the life of a bird.

To choose responsibly we require principles of judgment and calculation that are incompatible with viewing all living things as absolute values. To guide us here Aldo Leopold offers the image of the biotic pyramid beginning with the soil and proceeding through insects, plants, birds, and rodents, to the larger carnivores, and finally to humanity. Energy from the sun flows upward through the pyramid. "Evolution is a long series of self-induced changes, the net result of which has been to elaborate the flow mechanism and to lengthen the circuit."[2] Thus the evolutionary process, when we do not interfere, works toward maximization of the pyramid by both building the soil and multiplying the variety and complexity of the forms of life it supports.

Our interference in most places and at most times has reversed this process by impoverishing the soil and reducing the complexity of the biotic pyramid. To extend concern to all living things calls us to work with rather than against the evolutionary process. We must adapt our actions so that both the base and the complexity of the biotic pyramid may again grow, both for our own sake and for the sake of other species of which it is composed.

The new Christianity must substitute a vision of a healthy biotic pyramid with humanity at its apex for the absoluteness of human beings. This negation of the sacredness of human life is not without biblical grounds. Indeed, in its purest form prophetic faith has affirmed that only God is sacred or absolute. That doctrine *can* have profoundly negative consequences by reducing us and all creation to mere instruments of God. Humanism has often been justified in criticizing certain types of theism for their depreciation of human value. But if God is understood as concerned for and involved in the whole evolutionary process culminating in humanity, then these negative consequences can be avoided. In that case, renewal of the biblical vision of God as alone sacred would undergird and direct appropriate action in God's world.

A Style of Life for the Survival of Life

Through much of its history Christianity has advocated asceticism. The sense of the superior importance of spirit in relation to body has led to the attempt to concentrate all attention on perfecting spirit. Concern for the body has sometimes been condemned. It has even been thought that the spirit was directly benefited by denial of the body or even by the imposition of suffering upon it.

We have largely outgrown that kind of asceticism. We recognize more clearly today than in much of our Christian past that spirit and body jointly constitute one person, that both are good, that God is concerned for both, and that it is the total person who is to be forgiven and made whole. We recognize also that the world is good and that its enjoyment is good. Nothing is unclean in itself. God wants happiness and not misery. We particularly realize that the deeply entrenched view of sex as unclean and requiring special conditions for the justification of its practice is false. Sex is, or can be, a good and beautiful part of natural and wholesome life. Justification is required for restrictions placed upon it, not for its free expression.

As the rigors of Christian asceticism subsided, an economic asceticism emerged. It required hard work to earn enough of the world's goods to raise a family. One must work still harder and be even more careful in one's expenditures if one is to save. Only with savings can one have capital, and only with capital can one advance economically. Hence frugality is a major virtue, and waste, a major sin.

Those of us who lived through the depression will readily understand this kind of asceticism. But in the years since World War II it also has faded in the industrialized world and especially in our own country. Immense economic expansion has occurred, and its encouragement has been regarded as a major virtue. The expansion has been based on free borrowing and free spending on ever new products. Goods are manufactured to last only a few years so that they may be thrown away and replaced with newer and presumably better ones. Of course, none of us are ever able to buy all that we would like to own. Hence few of us feel fully part of the community of affluence. But almost all of us are spending freely on goods we would have learned to do without in the years of depression and World War II. In this context, economic asceticism is no longer a virtue. At most it is an occasional necessity imposed on some of us from time to time.

But as we face the fact of the finitude of the world's resources and the frightening pollution that is being caused by the present pace of production and consumption, we must move forward to a new asceticism, an ecological asceticism. We must find ways of reducing our destruction of the environment and of making irreplaceable resources last longer. Where shall we begin?

The obvious place to begin is with war and the preparation for war. From an ecological point of view nothing is more wasteful and destructive. Indeed, it is our preparations for war that have most clearly brought the whole question of survival to the fore. If we could reduce by half the production of war material, destroy all of our apocalyptic weapons, and cease to use our destructive power on the people and land of Third World, we would make immense strides toward bringing our national consumption of the world's resources and our national contribution to the destruction of the planet within reasonable limits.

But much, much more than this must be done. One large area is that of transportation. Our present system of transportation, in which we use two or three hundred horse power to transport one or two people everywhere they go, hastens the exhaustion of irreplaceable resources of gasoline and iron, poisons the air we breathe so that even plants cannot survive, and adds massively to the problem of disposal of solid wastes. Something drastic must be done quickly. Those of us who live in Southern California have already lost an average of a year or two from our lives because of the smog we breathe. The rest of the nation is not far behind.

Obviously much can be done. The Europeans and Japanese have long showed us how we can transport ourselves only a little less luxuriously with much less gasoline. But Detroit has largely ignored this possibility, and it is too late now for such halfway measures. We must either ban the internal combustion engine or achieve technical miracles in its performance, which until recently Detroit was not even willing to attempt. Meanwhile, we must make private transportation unattractive in relation to public transportation. This can be done by heavily taxing the former and heavily subsidizing the latter. An additional thirty percent tax on private automobiles and on gas, combined with turning freeways into toll ways, would raise enough money in California to provide comfortable and rapid public transportation. This should be inexpensive or even free. We could then almost stop construction of new highways. These may sound like drastic steps. But they are in fact very moderate in relation to the problem.

We also need to go into a new kind of city planning based on proximity of residence, work, and shopping, convenient public transportation, the encouragement of walking and bicycle riding, and the virtual elimination of private automobiles. New construction should be built upward on land already committed to housing, and further inroads on agricultural and wilderness lands should virtually cease. We should experiment with the mile-high cities envisioned by Paolo Soleri.

With regard to our irreplaceable resources, a strict policy on lumbering should be instituted to insure that no further reduction of forests be tolerated and that substantial reforestation occur every year. If this leads to shortages of wood and wood products, these should not be made up by imports. On the contrary, the price of such products should rise sufficiently to discourage their use and to encourage recycling. Similarly, irreplaceable metals should be heavily taxed to discourage their use and encourage the development of substitutes. In general, the cost of new products in relation to repairs on old ones should be increased and the cost of water and electricity to the point where we would all be less wasteful.

Since it seems likely that large agricultural surpluses will be needed in the years ahead to meet crises in Latin America, Africa, and Asia, full-scale production should be encouraged. However, this should be done with drastically reduced use of insecticides and chemical fertilizers. If this reduces yield per acre, so be it. New methods of farming less dependent on chemicals can be devised. Temporary shortages will not be critical in comparison with the devastation that continued indiscriminate use of chemicals can work. Most of us could tighten our belts a little without damage to our health.

If you think that these proposals would raise costs without raising salaries, you are quite right. That is part of the purpose. If we can afford to buy less, we will do without. Especially, we can do without automobiles. But we could also reduce our present consumption of water, electricity, metal, and wood products. If repair shops were available we could continue to use many of the appliances we now discard in favor of new ones. Life would not be unbearable!

There should be a quick end to what we now know as garbage collection. In its place would be a system of separate collections of each type of waste that can be recycled or converted into organic fertilizer. Such collection should be free. On the other hand, a high charge should be placed on the disposal of unusable waste.

Some system must be devised for encouraging industry to concentrate on the production of high quality, long lasting, easily repaired goods rather than to continue the present planned obsolescence. The whole system of new styles, and of advertising intended to create dissatisfaction with serviceable equipment, must be discouraged and resisted.

All of this would cause some economic dislocation, and the easing of hardships caused thereby should be a major national priority. Total production for the private sector would be somewhat reduced, although the higher quality demanded and the increased emphasis on repairs could prevent reduction in the number of people employed. There would be ample place for the exertion of energies diverted from overproduction. Enormous expenditures will be necessary. It will be extremely costly in goods and services merely to stop the increase of pollution of our waterways. To clear up those already polluted will cost more.

In this country, my proposals would lead to considerable reduction in the consumption of petroleum products and some reduction in the consumption of electricity. They also would require relative stability of consumption in other industrialized nations. This would enable these countries to convert gradually and cautiously to the use of other sources of energy as the supply of fossil fuels declines. Use of atomic energy should be expanded only if more adequate provisions can be made for disposition of wastes and heat. The use of solar energy, geothermal energy, and energy from ocean waves appears to be ecologically safer. If we can experiment without the pressure of urgency, safe long-term sources of energy may be harnessed.

It may be too much to hope that the underindustrialized nations will be cautious about the ecological consequences of their development. We can hardly ask these nations to husband resources carefully after the pattern of exploitation we have set. Even so, if we begin to set a new example ourselves and to be more generous and wise in our assistance, improvement is possible.

While affluent Americans learn to consume less, levels of consumption in some segments of American society should be increased. Shifting from expensive private cars to subsidized public transportation would be one step toward improving the lot of the poor. But much else must be done.

Whereas in the past we have employed our surplus wealth for industrial expansion and the purchase of additional goods, we should now put the emphasis on services. We have been voting down money for schools so as to buy a second car, or add a backyard swimming pool, or redecorate our homes. We must reverse this. Education is ecologically cheap. We should refrain from further expansion of our total industrial plant and put our resources instead into improving the ratio of teachers to students in our schools. Especially the children of the disadvantaged should be provided with numerous well-paid teachers. These should be given all possible encouragement by the community to experiment with ways of overcoming these children's handicaps. We can expand work in the mental health field as well. The arts also should be subsidized and encouraged. In all these areas services should be free or inexpensive. If we must learn gradually to be satisfied with fewer and less elegant goods, we can reasonably ask that these be replaced with services designed to enrich the life of the mind, deepen self-understanding, and improve human relations. Revenue from the high taxes designed to discourage waste of metals, wood products, electricity, and water can subsidize education, mental health, and the arts.

I introduced this discussion by speaking of a new, ecological asceticism. Yet the style of life I have sketched is hardly ascetic by past standards. Indeed, viewed in perspective, the change from the present affluent life is not immense. We could make these changes if we wanted.

The real question is whether they would be sufficient. They would certainly slow down our consumption of irreplaceable resources, make possible some increase in recreational lands, forests, and wilderness, and greatly reduce pollution. But the remaining rate of consumption would still involve ecologically harmful practices, and irreplaceable resources would still be used in large quantity. More drastic measures might be required.

This chapter has considered the American situation. Most of the other industrial nations may not need to reduce so greatly their level of consumption, but changes will be required of all of them. Their major need may be only to abandon their visions of a continuing increase in production. Something near the present level of economic activity in Japan and Europe might serve as a satisfactory norm for the long term. The world's task, its Herculean labor, is to bring the unindustrialized nations up toward this standard of life. This *cannot* be accomplished unless population is stabilized or reduced. Even then it *may* be impossible without ecological catastrophe. But we must try. A stable and generous America could do much to help.

Too Many People—The Ethical Problem

When it comes to proposals like those in the previous chapter, there will certainly be objections. Some will regard them as unrealistic and excessive. Some will oppose the further restrictions on laissez-faire capitalism. Others will regard them as entirely insufficient and far too moderate in their implications for our economic system. But few would oppose them as immoral or incompatible with fundamental ethical principles.

However, none of our efforts will be of much avail unless the total population of the nation is stabilized. Suppose that by measures of the sort suggested, we succeeded over a twenty-year period in reducing per capita consumption of goods (not services) by twenty-five percent. This would require somewhat more than a twenty-five percent decrease on the part of the majority to allow for a very much needed increase on the part of the now underprivileged. That would be an impressive achievement when we consider that it would require a reversal of all existing trends! Nevertheless, a modest population growth of just over one percent annually would wipe it out. Our total national consumption of the Earth's resources in 1990 would still be at its present ecologically unacceptable level.

On the other hand, if we did reduce our per capita consumption while stabilizing our population, we could both improve our environment and make major contributions to other peoples in their struggle to achieve a decent mode of life. In the nonindustrialized countries we could give priority to programs designed to achieve population stability and in some cases reductions. If this occurred, then twenty years from now the planet might not be twenty years nearer the extinction of life but instead be moving toward an era of stability and a balance with the environment that might endure. Surely the latter is the more attractive prospect.

But talk of population stability has profound moral implications. Some who think of each individual human life as having absolute value believe that the more lives the better. For them, the quality of the individual life is a secondary consideration. That is an extreme view. But even if few advocate it in just those terms, it influences the thought of many. If it is correct, then we should seek the largest possible population for the planet, be indifferent to the extermination of other forms of life, and accept the relative misery of the crowded individuals. If people hold to this principle, we can deter them from pushing for rapidly increasing population only by showing that this backfires, that the attempt to increase the population will bring on wars, famines, and pestilences that will in fact reduce it. And if they believe that God or nature is on the side of such increase they will be even more difficult to convince. They will expect the unexpected. They may even talk of peopling other planets as our vocation!

To those who think in these terms there is no moral justification for discouraging or preventing births. In their view the attempt to do so expresses a selfish desire to enjoy the economic advantages and personal freedom that small families make possible. Or else it expresses a fundamental failure to appreciate the absolute value of human life and the accompanying reduction of all other things to their instrumental value.

Action expressing these principles would be self-defeating. Humanity does not have the choice of rapid increase of population over a long period of time. The planet cannot support us. More people can survive longer if measures are taken promptly to prevent such increase of population. The importance of the vision within which one operates appears again at this point. One who believes in population growth as a good for its own sake will yield on each point only when it is unequivocally necessary to do so. Compromise of that sort will inevitably be too little and too late.

The alternative principle to which I have appealed is the reverence for all life. Those who live by this vision will seek a balance and harmony between as many forms of life as possible. Of course they will unhesitatingly choose human life over any other form when the choice is to be made. But they will favor restraint on humanity's part. The annihilation of other species need not occur so frequently. We can work with the total movement of life on the planet rather than destroy all but the human portion and that most obviously necessary to us. Birth control will be the single most important expression of the needed restraint.

Birth control can be encouraged in many ways. Women must be given opportunities for fulfilling vocations other than motherhood. Sex education should be mandatory in our schools. A social stigma would be attached to large families in the future. Contraceptives should be cheap and accessible. Tax laws should make more than two children financially unattractive. Once we have accepted the moral importance of stabilizing population, such measures will be clearly appropriate.

From a practical point of view, in an industrialized nation these are the most important measures. But in this chapter we are focusing on ethical issues and their relation to basic conviction, attitude, or consciousness. In this connection, the issue of abortion is especially important and interesting. It is not without its practical importance for controlling population. It has been extensively used in Japan and Eastern European countries in their successful efforts to limit population and it may be necessary elsewhere. Even in our nation, although other means will play the dominant role, abortion may also be important. There are still hundreds of thousands of unplanned and unwanted babies born in the United States every year. Legal, inexpensive abortions will help to reduce the number.

Recently the argument for abortion has centered around the rights of the mother. Should the state force a woman to carry to term an unwanted fetus? Only now is the further question being asked: To help achieve population stability should society discourage the bearing of unwanted children?

One way of approaching such a question is purely pragmatic and social. We might assume that the end to be sought is a smoothly functioning and happy society. We might then decide on policies with respect to abortion solely in terms of their contribution to this end. However, such a position would violate strong convictions about what is right and wrong. These include elements of absoluteness that stand in tension with purely pragmatic considerations about the welfare of society.

The idea of something being absolute was introduced in chapter 6. There "absolute" was treated as the secular equivalent of "sacred." When something is viewed as sacred, or as absolute in this sense, it is excluded from evaluation in terms of further consequences.

In the dominant Western tradition the destruction of a fetus is absolutely wrong *if* the fetus is "human." But how can one decide when the organism becomes "human"? Some have suggested that it is human when it is first capable of life separate from the mother. Others date the humanity from quickening. Still others have pushed back the date to conception itself. But all such decisions are arbitrary, since there are no sudden breaks or abrupt departures in the development from fertilization to birth.

The problem can be solved by a step that was proposed in chapter 6. If we give up the sense of absoluteness or sacredness with respect to human life, the question of when the fetus becomes human is no longer decisive. We are free to adjust our view of the humanity of the organism to the evidence and state that the process of development is one in which distinctively human traits gradually emerge both in the womb and after birth. Then, although by some definitions the unfertilized ovum is already human and by others even a saint is not yet fully human, such diversity of definitions will be acceptable because no moral absolutes hinge upon discovering the *true* or *correct* definition. If the human is not sacred or absolute, then the prohibition against taking innocent human life is not absolute either. That it is worse to destroy a child ready to be born than a newly fertilized ovum is not denied, but this now becomes a matter of degree.

Earlier I contrasted our tendency to see some moral principles as absolute with a vaguely indicated norm of social welfare. One profound danger of liberating ourselves from absolutes is that we may then allow the good of society to become the sole criterion of right and wrong. The worth and rights of the individual are then subordinated to the society, and the individual is judged in terms of instrumental value to the whole. If the society finds some of its members undesirable, it is then morally free to liquidate them. In that direction lie the gas chambers of Dachau.

Fortunately, we need not and should not choose between treating individuals as absolute and subordinating the individual to the societal good. The alternative to this choice can be stated in the distinction between intrinsic and instrumental value. Something has intrinsic value when its existence is good in itself, that is, regardless of any consequences or uses it may have for others. In this sense, a joyful experience is intrinsically valuable. A pencil, on the other hand, has negligible intrinsic value. Its existence matters very little apart from its use. The pencil has instrumental value, that is, it helps people to achieve greater intrinsic values.

The joyous experience is not only an intrinsic value; it also has instrumental value. It may have a beneficial effect on subsequent bodily health. It is likely to make one, for a time, a pleasanter companion. It enriches subsequent experiences through being remembered. In such ways every intrinsic value also has instrumental value, but many instrumental values have negligible intrinsic value.

Intrinsic value can be found in experience and experience alone. Generally, Westerners have supposed that it is found only in *human* experience. Against this limitation I have argued above and will argue further. But the limitation of intrinsic value to experience is sound, and experience always belongs to someone or something. Hence society as a whole, or the state, has instrumental value only. It is to be judged as it contributes to the increase of intrinsic value in the actual experiences it affects. To transpose absolute value from individual human beings to a corporate body like the state is, therefore, in no way justified by the general rejection of absolutes. On the contrary, individuals are the one locus of intrinsic value, and the state is to be judged by its contribution to them.

Corresponding to the idea of intrinsic value as distinct from absolute value is the idea of principles that always have moral weight when they are applicable. Telling the truth is an example. In making an ethical decision as to what to say, one cannot ignore the obligation to tell the truth. But if one must lie to save an innocent human life, the principle that innocent people are to be saved may well outweigh the other. On the other hand, if one could save an innocent human life only at the expense of condemning many to misery, another principle about enhancing the wider good might outweigh it. In these examples no one principle is absolute; all have intrinsic validity.

The principle that innocent human life should be preserved is a special case, as Schweitzer says, of the principle that all life should be saved. This is certainly not an absolute principle. But it means that no life should be destroyed idly or without cause. Thus there is an important ethical principle counting against the destruction of a fetus at any stage in its development whether or not the most useful definitions of "human" include it. This means that to consider *only* the casual preference of the mother or some slight benefit to society at large as grounds for destruction of a fetus is to violate the principle.

But there are also other principles. The mother's happiness or the general advantages for people not directly involved should *also* be considered. To consider *only* the principle of saving life would violate these and other important principles. The complexity of moral decision results from the complexity of relations among the many principles that demand consideration. None of these principles are absolute. When the situation is viewed in the light of the dangers to all the higher forms of life that result from planetary overpopulation, the outcome of responsible moral reflection will sometimes be more favorable to abortion than when this factor is left out of account.

However, there is an important practical argument against shifting the ethical consideration of abortion from the realm of absolutes to the realm of weighing conflicting valid principles. The taboo on the destruction of innocent human life from conception to natural death has served the West well. It has given more people more security in their persons than any other society has enjoyed. Its extension around the world has been in most respects a blessing, despite the population explosion to which it has contributed. If the taboo is removed at one point, how can it be held at others? If a fetus may be destroyed, may not an unwanted newborn child also be killed, especially if it is deformed or diseased? Will not euthanasia be approved and the efforts to keep the aged alive relaxed? What about the insane and the hopelessly ill? Finally, what about all those who are a drain on society and those whose genetic contribution to the race is undesirable? If there are too many people, can we not reduce the population selectively in favor of the healthy and intelligent?

Each of these questions has to be faced seriously, but this is not the place. Certainly the removal of an absolute taboo could have many bad consequences. It could lead to casual indifference to individual human life, whereas what we need is much more sensitive concern for the individual than we now show. One reason for urging population stabilization is that if the total population becomes too great this concern for individual life will be further weakened. Individuals will be viewed more and more as ciphers and less and less as persons.

To avoid the dangerous consequences, we need to emphasize another principle. All persons should be assured of the support of the community in living as long as they desire to live. Of course, that is not an absolute principle either. There seem to be times when killing a human being who desires to live is justified. But we should require a great deal of justification before destroying the life of one who wants to live, more justification than is now required, and not less. Our task is to undergird and deepen a genuinely personal concern for each individual without absolute taboos.

Nature as Historic

John F. Kennedy wrote: "For the first century after independence, we regarded the natural environment as indestructible—and proceeded vigorously to destroy it."[1] The struggle to change that attitude, and thus to reverse that practice, is far from completed.

In the preceding chapters I described the objective problem we face and some of the steps needed to deal with it. Again and again it was made clear that we must not merely do different things, but must also regard the natural environment in a new way, adopt a fresh attitude, and alter the principles in terms of which we make our decisions.

But we cannot make these changes by a simple act of will. We cannot simply *decide* to love nonhuman entities. We can do so only if these entities appear to us as appropriate objects of love. As yet, most expressions of love toward the nonhuman world seem naive and sentimental. To enter into those expressions ourselves goes against deeply ingrained habits and fundamental assumptions. It goes against our basic vision of reality.

Consider, for example, how we feel about the two men mentioned in chapter 6 as embodying the new Christianity we need to adopt. Francis of Assisi is greatly admired throughout Christendom, but we smile condescendingly at his behavior toward birds and animals. Schweitzer is widely recognized as one of the great men of the twentieth century, but we are a little embarrassed by just that behavior of his which shows that he took seriously the principle of reverence for all life. We tolerate these strange actions as the pardonable foibles of a saint and genius.

As long as our vision remains estranged from theirs, it is useless to pretend to adopt their attitudes. If we do not see the nonhuman world as real and valuable in its own right, to love it is sentimental nonsense. The remainder of this chapter and the next three are devoted to overcoming elements in the orthodox view that block disinterested concern for the nonhuman world.

The universe is mostly a vast, almost empty, expanse of space-time. Scattered through it in an uneven but not quite random way are innumerable stars. Around some of these revolve satellites that we call planets. One of these planets revolving around a star of modest size is alive. We call that planet Earth.

Perhaps there are other living planets circling other stars in this or other galaxies. But the conditions requisite for any high grade of life to appear are far more special and complex than is often recognized. A planet must be neither too large nor too small, neither too heavy nor too light, and neither too close nor too distant from its star. Its development must occur in a definite and by no means inevitable sequence. Suitable mutations must appear at particular times.

Even if life has appeared elsewhere in the universe, it is highly unlikely that it has used the same amino acids or the same genetic code. Even if somewhere it has chanced to do so, there is no reason to suppose that it would have followed a line of development culminating in creatures similar to us. There is no necessity in the emergence of mammals or primates. There is nothing about primates that insures the evolutionary emergence of man. The primates of the New World would never have evolved in this way.

The other planets in our solar system are presumed lifeless. We know nothing of life elsewhere in the universe. In an area to be measured by hundreds of light years, if not in all the infinities of space, we are alone.

This planet has not always been alive. Indeed, as Richard Overman[2] has recently reminded us, if we conceive the five billion years of the Earth's past as though recorded in ten volumes of five hundred pages each, so that each page records a million years, cellular life appears only somewhere around the eighth volume, about a billion years ago. The story of all the plants and animals of the Cambrian period occupies only the tenth volume, and of this, the first half is taken up with how plants became terrestrial and the amphibians emerged. Around page 440 of this 500-page book the reptiles reach the height of their development, and it is not until page 465 that their dominance is superseded by that of birds and warm-blooded animals. Finally, on page 499 of this tenth volume the human species appears. The last two words on the last page recount our story from the rise of civilization six thousand years ago until the present.

Throughout the last two volumes life proliferated, creating an environment in which more complex forms of life could emerge and prosper. Both life and the capacity to support life increased millennia after millennia. Humans entered the scene on a planet that was biologically very rich indeed. To that organic richness we contributed little. In fact, in certain localities over limited periods of time our treatment of the environment was quite destructive. But only when we reach the last letter of the last word on the last page do we turn the tide against life. Only then do we begin the process of killing the planet. What is astonishing is that all that has been produced over the course of a billion years is so vulnerable to destruction by this late-latecomer to the scene.

Yet it should not surprise us that what takes so long to create can be so easily destroyed. It took only a moment for an assassin's bullet to destroy the complex richness of the life of a John F. Kennedy or a Martin Luther King. That richness of thought, will, and feeling had been many years in the making, but it depended on an organic base that could be destroyed almost instantaneously. The life of the planet similarly depends on a physical base which, now that we have mastered its secrets, is vulnerable to our destruction. For at least a hundred years, and with everquickening acceleration, we have been destroying it. The eleventh volume may recount the much poorer story of a lifeless planet.

This perspective on ourselves is important because of the profound illusions we Westerners, and especially we Americans, have entertained about our natural environment. We have supposed, consciously or unconsciously, that it is inexhaustible and indestructible. Of course, we have known that a few species of wildlife were becoming extinct and that here and there we had turned fertile fields into dust bowls, but these we felt were isolated phenomena having nothing to do with our basic situation. We thought that we could learn lessons from our mistakes and through ever-increasing scientific knowledge and technological skill advance to new heights of prosperity and comfort. We might worry about the loss of some prized moral and spiritual values, but our pictures of future life were always in terms of fantastic progress in science and technology. In this scenario, nature was cast in the role of supplier of limitless resources for our use and enjoyment.

Now we are discovering that our assault upon nature, intended to wrest from it the materials for this technological utopia, is profoundly affecting its ability to serve us. Even with quite modest technology, our ancestors turned fertile land into the Sahara and Gobi deserts. Only an axe is required to expose forest soils to erosion and begin the all too rapid process of creating new wastelands. But today's science and technology introduce whole new means of changing the environment, and their results are far more rapid and drastic. Our means of producing the vast quantities of energy we need both heat and pollute the atmosphere in ways that may either bring on a new ice age or melt the Arctic ice. Our poisons, such as DDT, may kill birds and fish and even plankton, thereby disrupting the ecological cycles on which we, too, ultimately depend. Increase of radiation from the production of atomic energy, even without an atomic war, may alter the genetic character of many species of life including the human. Should another major war occur, it is human and animal life as such, and not merely its quality and character, that is threatened.

Our resistance to the full assimilation of these now well-known facts still stems in large part from our intellectual habits. Especially in Protestant circles, we have been taught to distinguish and contrast history and nature. In history, we suppose, things happen uniquely and irreversibly, whereas in nature they recur and repeat themselves endlessly. Thus history is the only locus of real change. Nature, we assume, will always be the same. In this view, the human, historical future is uncertain, but there is nothing to be anxious about so far as nature is concerned. It is infinite and eternal.

This dualism stems from the distinction between the two modes of investigation. Historians have concerned themselves with a narrative account of a sequence of unique and unrepeatable events. Scientists have sought laws which would hold good for all times and places. Yet even this distinction is grossly exaggerated. There are genetic sciences like geology as well as those seeking universal laws. And historians can and do make generalizations about nations, revolutions, and economic depressions.

Aldo Leopold has shown us that human history is itself deeply affected by a biotic succession humanity does not intend or control. When the forests of Kentucky were cut down, the lush bluegrass appeared. The settlers prospered. But when the American southwest was deforested and grazed, it became barren. Many of the settlers were forced to move on in order to survive. Thus the history of humanity and that of other forms of life are intertwined.

Yet contrary to all evidence, we have viewed the nonhuman world as existing solely for us—a fundamentally inexhaustible and changeless stage on which we are to play out our human drama. We have simply refused to see that the stage participates in the drama, and we are still reluctant to admit that it is beginning to collapse irreparably. Our exaggerated distinction between methods of inquiry in science and history has misled us into supposing that their objects—"natural" and "human" events—are fundamentally distinct and separable.

In this respect, the biblical vision was more accurate than the dominant modern one. The nonhuman world, although pictured on a smaller scale still appeared vast to ancient people. It was intimately involved in human history, sharing in the fall, suffering from human sin, and destined to share redemption in the end.

Today we would picture our role in the cosmic drama as important only in its very latest stages. But that the nonhuman world, too, has a history, and that this history is intimately bound up with ours so that both will suffer a common fate, is all too sadly true.

This view of nature as historic and contingent helps to awaken us to the full seriousness of the problem that we now face. It has another importance as well. It brings the nonhuman world closer to us so that by seeing how our fates are bound up together, by recognizing how much we are indebted to it and depend upon it, and by realizing how vulnerable it is to our actions and how deeply we have wounded it, we enter into a new consciousness. That consciousness nurtures warmer and more tender feelings. When we view living nature in all its innumerable forms as sharing with us in a precarious existence, and when we see the products of aeons of struggle threatened with extinction, we can no longer be indifferent.

Humanity as Part of Nature

In every religion what is sought with the help of the superhuman spiritual power reverenced by man, is a solution of the contradiction in which man finds himself, as both a part of the world of nature and a spiritual personality claiming to dominate nature. . . . In this juncture, religion springs up as faith in superhuman spiritual powers, by whose help the power which man possesses of himself is in some way supplemented, and elevated into a unity of its own kind which is a match for the pressure of the natural world.[1]

So wrote Albrecht Ritschl, the most influential Protestant theologian of the latter part of the nineteenth century. For him nature was something that pressed upon humanity, something that humanity was called upon to dominate. The function of religion was to assist in achieving this dominance. This separation of humanity from the rest of nature and this fundamentally negative attitude toward nature were all too typical of Protestant theology up to the time when awareness of the ecological crisis dawned.

One of the first theological books to be stimulated by the awareness of this crisis was Frederick Elder's *Crisis in Eden*. Elder sees one main theological issue, that is, the choice between the view of those like Ritschl whom he calls exclusionists and that of the inclusionists whom he supports. Exclusionists view humanity as outside of nature and in opposition to it. Inclusionists see humanity as within and part of nature.

Because the word nature has so rich a history and so varied a range of connotations, I have spoken often of the nonhuman world instead. Obviously, by definition, human beings are external to the nonhuman world, but that by no means settles the issue Elder is raising. That issue is how humans are related to the nonhuman world. Do they see themselves as separated from it by a radical discontinuity, or do they see themselves as continuous with it? Do they see their relation to everything else as fundamentally of a different order from the relation of other things to each other, or do they see their relation to the nonhuman world as a special case of the kinds of relations that exist within that world?

As examples of exclusionists, Elder uses his Harvard teachers Herbert Richardson and Harvey Cox. His example of an inclusionist is Loren Eiseley. It is instructive that he went outside the professional theological community to find an inclusionist. I wish that this had been unnecessary, that he could have chosen a theological naturalist. But the Christian tradition has been deeply committed to the exclusionist view.

I align myself with the inclusionists for two reasons. First, they are factually correct. Humanity evolved with and from the nonhuman world, and although it has crossed many thresholds in its development, none of them constitutes the sort of divide that would justify the exclusionist view. A human being's difference from a chimpanzee is analogous to a chimpanzee's difference from a sardine or a sardine's difference from an amoeba. These differences are vast, but they do not justify views of total discontinuity when the evidence of evolutionary continuity is so great.

Since most exclusionists today acknowledge the evolutionary connection, the factual argument is not to be pressed. But whereas they think that the fact of evolution is not important for fundamental human self-understanding, it seems to me of great importance. They focus attention on some special aspect of human beings, such as reason, self-consciousness, or speech. They hold that however this came into being, it now marks human beings off decisively from all other forms of life. The factual question between us, then, is the separability of that distinctive aspect of the human from the rest of human being and its discontinuity with the nonhuman world. Here the argument is often complex and dependent on philosophical assumptions.

Therefore it will be better to stress my second reason for favoring inclusionism which is that it will further that next step in the development of Christian existence for which I called in chapter 6. There I suggested that whereas Christianity has thus far urged us to have concern for all our fellow human beings, we need now to extend our concern to the whole of life. Only if we do this will we take those actions which will insure our own survival.

As Christians we speak more often of love than of concern or reverence. But there are many kinds of love. Within the family there is the love between husband and wife, the love between parents and children, and the love among the children. Freud has taught us to recognize an erotic element in all human relations, but this is most clearly and best symbolized in the love between husband and wife. This kind of love has played a large role in religions and it is affirmed and approved by Christianity. But it is not the kind of love we are called to extend to all human beings and beyond. This universal love is better symbolized as sibling love. In the ideal relation between siblings there is no possessiveness or attempt to achieve intense feelings of relatedness. There is an acceptance of siblings as fellow human beings who are to go their own way as quite separate and independent persons. But there is also concern for their welfare and recognition of responsibility to them and for them.

Christianity has accentuated the nonerotic character of the love for which it calls by stressing that it is to be directed especially toward the unattractive and unworthy. Jesus sought out the sick and the sinner rather than the healthy and the virtuous. It is not erotic attractiveness, but need, that governs the direction of active concern. Christian love does not seek to unite with its objects or to possess them. It seeks their good for their own sake and encourages their free and independent development.

But the image of sibling love also indicates that Christian love is based on a sense of similarity. Others are to be loved because they, like myself, are real subjects of feeling and action. In and of themselves they have the same claim to respect and concern as I have. To measure them in terms of their value to me is to ignore the reality in which I believe.

The sense of sharing a common status with all other people is fundamental to our Christian perspective. But in the past, it has tended to mark off a boundary at the line dividing humanity from other animals. The recognition of kinship has been limited to the human race. Since it is so difficult to make effective even this humanly inclusive sense of kinship against the pressures of racism and national- ism, the issue of its extension has rarely been raised.

Now, however, it is important for us to extend the range of respect and concern to nonhuman forms of life. But we cannot simply do this as an act of will. We can do it only as our vision, our sense of reality, changes. This will change only as we become vividly aware of kinship with other living things. We must come to experience ourselves as a part of that whole community of living things to which we point by speaking of the evolutionary process.

There is as much ground for inclusionism as for exclusionism in the Bible. The fateful story of creation represents human beings as created like the rest, from the dust of the earth. We are co-creature with fish and birds and beasts. The fundamental duality lies between creator and creature, not between the human species and other animals.

Yet the story speaks of God creating humans in the divine image, thus lifting them above the rest, and Christian theology has focused more upon the image of God than upon human co-creaturehood with other animals. It has given to the idea of the divine image in man and woman a prominence far greater than it is accorded in the Old Testament. It has thus led to a three-fold distinction of God, humanity and nature against the more basic biblical distinction of creator and creation. It is the image of co-creaturehood which we need now to recover without the loss of the biblical sense of humanity as the apex of creation.

In calling for Christians to take seriously humanity's inclusion within nature, I have implied that few theologians have done so. Yet much recent theology has stressed human bodiliness. It has opposed no less earnestly than I the dualism that treated human beings as purely mental somehow connected with a piece of machinery that they own and operate. Indeed, in contemporary theology it has become fashionable to assert that human beings are bodies. This doctrine seems quite close to the stressing of inclusion of humanity within nature. Just for this reason, the differences are important for the argument of this book. From the perspective of an inclusionist, I have two major objections to offer to the idea that humans *are* their bodies. Explaining them will help to make clearer what is involved and what is not involved in inclusionism.

The first objection to the doctrine that one is one's body is that if it were taken literally and seriously, the value and truth of the historic idea of the soul would be lost. If one quite unequivocally were one's body, then one would be one's corpse as well. However, those who adhere to this doctrine do not mean anything of this sort. For them, one is one's body functioning in all the dimensions in which the human body can function.

But even when in fairness we allow this qualification to be made, the doctrine is a dangerous one. If it means anything at all, then the excellence of the body and its functioning must be the basis on which people are rightly evaluated. The crippled and the blind are really inferior human beings. In so far as the body structures of various races are significantly different, the people belonging to those races are significantly different.

But these are not the consequences which the doctrine intends to support. Those who say that they *are* their bodies are stressing that they fully accept their bodiliness, refuse to treat their bodily needs and pleasures as inferior to other functions of their person, and give up all thought of a life beyond death separate from their bodies. But if their doctrine is accepted, the unintended consequences follow too—a doctrine is not innocent of its unintended consequences. If we really identify people as bodies, we will and should treat them as such. We will no longer attribute to them the kind of value we have accorded them in the past. There will be no basis for loving them unless we find their bodies and their actions attractive. There will be no idea of a deeper unity transcending differences of appearance. There will be no sense of the possibility of triumphing spiritually over the adversities of the body. Only if we distinguish a feeling and acting subject from the body and its behavior can we distinguish the worth of the person from the attractiveness or excellence of the body. Only then can we conceive the possibility that a cripple may be a better person than a beautiful athlete. Only then can we hold on to the lesson taught by Socrates.

To see ourselves as fully a part of nature does not entail these consequences. If nature were composed only of bodies, of course these results would follow. But nature contains many living beings that feel and act. We are not alone in being feeling and acting subjects who feel and act through the body without simply being bodies. We are alone in many of the dimensions of our feeling and acting, but our distinctiveness is that of a unique being within nature, not of a being outside nature.

The second objection is that the doctrine that we are our bodies assumes that the body is more unified in itself and separate from other things than it really is. When one takes this position one does not notice all the ways our bodies are involved with their environment. We appreciate our interconnection with the natural environment only when we see the body as something complex and distinct from the person.

The distinctness of a person from the body does not imply the kind of separateness and difference that Greeks and Christians have often affirmed. The evidence points to a relation that is far more intimate than that. Personal life grows out of the body and its experiences, and it expresses itself through the body. A person does not exist before the body or apart from the body. What one is as an experiencing and deciding subject, one is in intimate interrelation with one's body. But discrimination is required. One's relation to toenails is quite different from one's relation to the liver. One's relation to one's eyes differs from both. One's relation to a red corpuscle in one's blood differs from one's relation to a cancer cell in the chest or urine in the bladder. Most intimate is one's relation to the brain.

That these differences exist can easily be shown physiologically. A local anesthetic can alter the relation of the person to certain parts of the body. Also, persons are not much changed when their appendices are removed or when they give blood to the Red Cross. But they are profoundly changed if a substantial part of their brains are removed. These facts seem too obvious to mention. We may be told that a person's self-identification with the body has nothing to do with physiology. But against the unclarified doctrine of indiscriminate identity of person and body, a reminder is needed. A person is intimately involved with the body, but the degree of intimacy with different parts of the body differs. One is not one's body as such or in general.

Only when we recognize the diversity of relations within the body are we able to recognize adequately the continuity between a person's relations with the body and relations with the environment. In fact, we cannot specify a sharp boundary line between the body and its environment. When does a piece of meat cease being a part of the environment and become a part of the body? When it is swallowed? When it is digested? Or only later? Further, the relations of a person to parts of the environment are sometimes more intimate than relations to parts of one's own body. My personhood is often more shaped by the words I am hearing than by the skin on my left heel. In sexual intercourse a person's dependence on and intimacy with another body and another person is greater than the dependence on and intimacy with marrow in one's own bones or the hair on one's own head.

We should thus be warned against isolating the individual body as if it first existed and then interacted with other things. It is itself a complex web of interactions which are interacting with the environment. Both person and body are interdependent with the environment. But the person is distinct from the environment too. Interdependence is not the same as identity.

To know myself as within nature is to know that the ecological system of interpenetration and interdependence includes me, both my body and my personality. It is not to cease to think of myself as an individual person, but it is to cease to think of a person as existing prior to or independently of relations. These relations extend throughout the body and throughout the wider environment.

Is the Nonhuman World Real?

In the first eight chapters, we saw that we need a new attitude of love and concern for the nonhuman world. We can develop this new attitude only as a new vision emerges. In chapters 9 and 10 some elements of that new vision have been sketched. Instead of viewing nature as a changeless and inexhaustible context for human action, we see all life as a fragile achievement of evolutionary processes that can be readily upset by human interference. Instead of viewing ourselves as standing outside of nature, we see ourselves as an interconnected part of the natural system of interdependence.

These changes in vision help to reorient us in our attitude. But this reorientation faces a very fundamental obstacle to which we have not yet attended. In our dominant Western vision the nonhuman world often lacks reality in itself. Even when it is granted some reality, that reality is not the kind that would justify our love for it.

We have already considered how the biblical-Christian tradition has led to a depreciation of the nonhuman world. But the point we are now considering goes much further than that. Not only is the intrinsic *value* of the nonhuman world undercut, even its *reality* is questioned. At this point we have moved from theology to philosophy. The philosophical challenge to the inherent reality of the nonhuman world is certainly influenced by the theological challenge to its intrinsic value. But it is more radical. Unless we can believe in the world's reality, the question of its value cannot arise.

In order to consider this new matter, we have to think about what it means for something to be real. That is a very abstract or theoretical question. It is also very important, for our unconscious philosophical assumptions have a decisive bearing on our judgments and actions. But it is not easy to become conscious of these assumptions or even to understand what is being said about them.

Let us review briefly the oft-told story of modern Western philosophy from the point of view of the reality of the nonhuman world. No details are necessary. We begin, as is customary, with Descartes, who divided the world into minds and physical things. In so doing, he made a radical dualism of distinctions that had been present in both the Greek and the Christian traditions. He thereby forced a decision with respect to the status of animals, and he unhesitatingly placed them on the side of physical things. He attributed to them no feeling, no sensation, in short no subjectivity. They are to be viewed as machines, mere its.

Obviously, Descartes was influenced by aspects of his Christian heritage. Nevertheless, he was not merely reflecting the thought of his day. Instead, he was transforming it and thereby shaping the categories of the modern world. It is surely not without significance that the father of modern philosophy began by separating human beings metaphysically from all else in a way more drastic than had ever been done before in Western philosophy. In the process, he reduced everything else, the animate and the inanimate alike, to the status of mere bodies, whose major characteristic is that they are extended in space.

Descartes did at least allow the nonhuman world the status of *being.* Its substantiality seemed to him to reside in itself, independent of human observation. But as modern philosophy advanced, even the objective reality of the nonhuman came under searching questioning. The standpoint of inquiry was epistemological; that is, one asked what and how one can know. The inquiry began with human experience and resulted in equating reality with what people can experience or know. Approached in this way, the physical things of Descartes became sense data for subsequent philosophers. As sense data, they could no longer exist in themselves as substances. Since, nevertheless, sense data appear to the human mind as something *given,* Berkeley taught that an active mind other than the human must be their source. But if this is so, then trees and dogs do not exist as objects which can be appropriately loved. They are only the impressions that God's mind works on ours.

Berkeley attributed to God the power of presenting an ordered world of sense data to us. Kant attributed this power to human mind. In his thought the movement toward a completely human-centered view of reality thus takes yet one step more. He did not mean that we individually and voluntarily decide what order to project upon our environment. The order is settled by the structure of mind itself. This structure can be discovered by analyzing the projected order. Still "mind" means human mind, and that mind is almost entirely alone with itself. True, Kant allowed that there are in the environment other entities, which he called "noumena." But these entities are wholly outside time and space, and they have no causal relations with anything. Since nothing can be known or asserted of them, Kant's successors rejected them. It is also true that Kant retained faith in God as mind. But Kant's God was irrelevant to our experience of our environment, and with this deity, too, Kant's successors dispensed.

Kant's influence upon subsequent philosophy can hardly be exaggerated. Not only Hegel and German idealism, but also more recent philosophies, such as phenomenology and existentialism, share explicitly or implicitly the vision of the human mind alone with itself. They conceive this mind in highly diverse ways. Whereas for Kant it is static, Hegel sees it as developing through history. Whereas Kant attends to the structuring activity of mind, Husserl attends to the objects of mind. But for him, too, these objects remain the objects of *mind* and not objects as they might or might not exist in themselves apart from mind. Such "things-in-themselves" he brackets out of his philosophy. The existentialists go beyond Husserl in their understanding of human existence, but they have nothing to add with respect to how other things are in themselves.

Not all recent philosophy is Kantian. Most British philosophy went on its way little affected by Kant. Since it emphasized the sense data, it is usually called "empirical." It did not acknowledge so dominant a role for mind and tried to remain closer to the scientific study of the natural world. Yet, rather than providing a more helpful vision, its results are still more pernicious with respect to our need. The Kantians have at least maintained a sense of the reality and importance of the human mind, thus providing the ground for the concern of human beings for each other. But, the great empiricist Hume undermined the substantial reality of the mind as well. Although he is not entirely consistent, the implications of his thought leave us with a flux of sensuous forms and concepts devoid of being and value. Instead of lifting the nonhuman world into participation in the value of the human world, this empiricism dissolves the human one as well. The later result is a positivism in which all consideration of value is meaningless.

Against this background the ordinary language analysis that is now dominant in the English-speaking world is a relief. It is largely in the empirical tradition, but the paradoxical results of empiricism have lost their hold. Since the common language corresponds roughly with Aristotelian philosophy, the results of its analysis tend to return to that philosophic tradition. On the other hand, not surprisingly, the results of ordinary language analysis tend to be determined by the common sense of the culture whose language is analyzed. In this case, it is shaped chiefly by a post-Christian humanism. When ordinary language is the norm, many of the philosophical obstacles to the appropriation of the vision of the world as real and valuable are weakened. But ordinary language philosophy cannot itself produce the new vision we need.

Thomas Aquinas received from Aristotle a philosophy that accepted the full and independent reality of the nonhuman world. He developed this doctrine into a balanced account of the relation of humanity to the rest of nature, both in its resemblance and in its difference. His influence continued through the modern period in Roman Catholic circles. In a movement called Neo-Thomism, Thomas' realistic view vigorously entered the wider intellectual discussion. However, through its participation in that discussion Neo-Thomism has come to stress the creativity of the human mind in its perception of the nonhuman world and to depreciate the autonomous reality of that world—the things in themselves. Through this recent "transcendental" turn, much of contemporary Thomism has been assimilated into the idealist tradition.

One might suppose that the natural scientists would resist the dissolution of nature into human experience. Most of them share the naive belief that what they investigate is more independent of their knowledge than the dominant philosophic interpretation allows. Nevertheless, they have also contributed to the dissolution of nature's reality. Especially in the most advanced scientific disciplines, scientists deal with a body of interrelated laws that are mathematically formulated. The question of the reality of the world to which the laws apply does not arise. The theories *seem* to describe a world that exists objectively and independently. But sophisticated philosophical interpretations of these theories often deny what on the surface they seem to say.

In addition to idealism and empiricism there is also a widespread materialism.

This receives its most influential expression in Marxism, which against all the arguments of idealism and empiricism insists upon the objective and primary reality of the physical world. But that reality is named "matter," and Marxists do not see matter as an object of concern in itself. Its value is economic, and economic value is determined entirely by human needs and desires.

Non-Marxist forms of materialism usually ally themselves closely with the technological attitude. Whatever they mean by matter, they do not attribute to it any intrinsic value. The doctrine that all things are material is used more to disparage the human claim to intrinsic value than to extend that value to other living things. What is material is there to be used and manipulated, not to be cherished and revered.

The conclusion of this survey of the major schools of modern philosophy is that none of them have attributed significant reality to things in themselves. Some have thought of the nonhuman world as having some sort of purely physical, merely material, or wholly unknowable existence in itself. Others have denied even this. In either case, love or concern for our fellow creatures would be viewed as mere sentimentality.

For most purposes it would be necessary to stress the great differences among such philosophical traditions as idealism, empiricism, and materialism. But in this chapter and those that follow, it is their agreement that is important. They all deny significant reality to the nonhuman world. Where this one issue alone is in view, it will be convenient to refer to them jointly as "the dominant philosophy."

This terminology reminds us immediately that there are other strands in modern philosophy that have not acquiesced in so anthropocentric a view. In addition to the influence of Aristotelian, Thomistic, and common sense realism, there have been such diverse philosophies as those of Leibniz and Jonathan Edwards. Some forms of romanticism have stressed the reality and value of all of nature. The rise of the evolutionary perspective in the nineteenth century encouraged new forms of naturalism, of which Bergson's thought is influentially representative. The naturalistic tradition in America partly avoids the dominant anthropocentrism. Heidegger has devoted his philosophical career to the reopening of the question of being. Teilhard de Chardin and Alfred North Whitehead will be discussed in the chapters that follow as recent spokesmen of this subdominant tradition which does attribute reality and value to the nonhuman world.

The isolation of humanity that is implied by the dominant philosophy has deeply affected the modern sensibility. Heidegger describes the experience of the human being as thrown into the world rather than as at home within it. Sartre writes of nausea. For a century alienation in its many forms has been a major motif of modern literature, and the alienation of humanity from the natural environment is basic to much of this experience.

But we may still ask how important is it to the "man in the street" that the dominant philosophy has denied significant reality to the nonhuman world. He has not studied philosophy, or at least not in such a way as to be much affected by it directly. He thinks quite naively of the reality of the objects he encounters. Can we not simply bypass the philosophical discussion and call on him to accept the significant reality and intrinsic value of the nonhuman world and to extend concern to it?

The answer is that indirectly, but pervasively, we are shaped by philosophy. Indeed, impressive testimony to the power of philosophical ideas over ordinary thinking is found in the writings of those most concerned about defending the environment from further ravages. One senses in these writings a deep feeling for the goodness of the world we have not altered, for the rights of animals to have the chance to survive, for the evil of inflicting unnecessary suffering upon them. But when one studies their arguments, one finds nothing said of all this. Apparently the defenders of the nonhuman world are not free to give conceptual expression to their real feelings and convictions. Marsh says of himself that as a boy, "The bubbling brook, the trees, the flowers, the wild animals were to me persons, not things." [1] This certainly cannot be considered irrelevant to his lifelong concern for the preservation and improvement of the good earth, or to his deep sensitivity to the interconnectedness of living things that enabled him to see so much that others overlooked. But his arguments for conservation are based on its importance *for human beings*.

The same is true of nature's defenders today. They argue that wilderness should be protected because of what it does *for us*. We need to be able occasionally to escape the noise, confusion, and artificiality of civilization and renew ourselves in a world we never made. The preservation of animal species is justified on the ground that we may yet learn new secrets from them that will benefit us. We may learn how to avoid arthritis from the now-threatened wolverine, since almost alone among animals, the wolverine is free from this disease. Cruelty to animals is undesirable because it breeds bad habits. Those who begin by being cruel to animals, end by being cruel to other persons as well.

Why the deep hesitation to affirm that there is value in wilderness in itself, that biological species are inherently worth preserving, and that individual animals have a right to happiness? The answer lies in part in the Christian centering of all intrinsic value in humanity. But it lies also in the philosophical denial of significant reality to things in themselves. The Christian tradition cannot transform itself by the extension of concern beyond human beings to fellow creatures without first overcoming the extreme anthropocentrism of its dominant philosophical positions.

The Philosophical Problem

None of the dominant forms of Western philosophy attribute significant reality to things in themselves. But Christian love is love for others as it is in itself. It is not based on how the other appears or functions, how it helps or harms the lover, or how it contributes to the general good. If we are to extend Christian love beyond the human circle, we must challenge the dominant philosophy and break the hold it has upon common sense. That is a large task.

To challenge the dominant philosophy we must first understand more clearly why it takes the position it does. A simple example will help. I see a chair. I can also feel that it exists. But when I say that the chair exists, what am I really saying? Am I speaking of something that I cannot see or feel, some thing-in-itself outside of my experience and in principle not subject to being experienced? The dominant philosophy denies that I can mean anything of this sort. By the chair, I mean just what I have experienced and can experience, as it is or may be in my experience. All that I mean by the chair is thus the chair *for me* or the chair *for people in general.*

It is recognized that "the man in the street" tends to think in naively realistic terms. He tends to think of the reality of the things he experiences as being independent of his experience. They are there, and then he happens to experience them. Some philosophers have agreed with this. But so far as they belong to the dominant school, they have noted that when we have said the object is there whether it is experienced or not, that it is there as a thing-in-itself, we have said all that can be said or thought about it. Everything else we say expresses how the object appears *to us.* Even to say that "something is there" is full of difficulties. It is hard to know what we mean in that apparently simple sentence by "something," by "is," and by "there." It is hard to think of any connection between this thing-in-itself and the thing-for-us.

One connection that seems plausible at first sight is the connection of cause and effect. We might think that the chair in itself *causes* my experience of it. But this idea, too, raises many difficulties and is generally rejected. Let us see why.

The dominant philosophy assumes that sense perception is the fundamental way in which we are related to the world. It is the starting point and basis for all our knowledge of the world. If there are other feelings, such as feelings of what is going on inside our bodies, these are to be understood as like our sensations of what is going on outside. Seeing something is the usual instance of experience that is analyzed in philosophy, and hearing and touching and tasting are assumed to be very much the same.

If experience is basically sense perception, then its objects can only be the peculiar and appropriate objects of sense perception—sense data, or perceived objects. Seeing gives us visual objects. Some think of these as patches of color. Others stress that they are colored *things,* but they do not mean colored things-in-themselves. A thing-in-itself could not be colored, since what we mean by color depends on its being seen. No matter how we come at the chair, all that we can experience of it are sense data.

Sense data can be the basis of making predictions. If I have the visual experience that I call seeing a chair, I anticipate that if I move closer and put out my hand, I will also have the tactile sensations I call touching the chair; and if I sit down, I expect to be supported. The chair is not identified with any one of these experiences. Rather what we mean by the chair has to do with all of them and with an indefinite number of other possible experiences. Again we come easily upon the idea that the unit underlying all of these varied experiences is the chair-in-itself, that the chair-in-itself is their cause.

But what do we mean here by "cause"? That is a much more difficult idea than is usually supposed. We need to take an example, and for the dominant philosophy, the standard examples come from the physical sciences and from ordinary language about the physical world. The following is a good example: Heat causes water to expand. Our question is whether the relation of the chair-in-itself to the chair-for-us can be conceived as being like the relation of heat and the expansion of water. To decide that, we have to become very clear as to what we mean by heat *causing* the expansion of water.

First, let us note what it does *not mean*. It does not mean that heat is some kind of an agent, like a man, which makes the water do something. No, what heat means here is the increase of temperature. The increase of temperature is measured by certain instruments, such as thermometers. To say that heat causes water to expand is to say that when the readings on the thermometers go up, we can observe that the volume of water also increases. Now we are back in the sphere of sense perception. We are speaking of a correlation between meter readings and other observable phenomena. There causal relations can be affirmed.

But if cause-and-effect is a relation between observable phenomena, then it is very different from the supposed relation between the unobserved and unobservable chair-in-itself and the chair-for-us. That relation remains just as unknowable and as unthinkable as the chair-in-itself. So once again we seem to have a good reason for forgetting all about things-in-themselves. They are entirely useless for the explanation of experience, and we have no reason to talk about them at all except for experience. There is human experience and there is the world as we experience it. About the world as it is in itself, there is nothing to be said.

I have given a very simple model of the dominant philosophy. What I have said is widely accepted in general, although each philosopher would want to restate it to bring out the proper nuance as she or he sees it. This matter of nuance is very important and leads to great differences among philosophers on many subjects. For the most part, however, it does not lead to a reopening of the question about whether we can have more knowledge about things-in-themselves. It is this widespread negative agreement that I have been trying to bring out.

Up to this point in this chapter, we have been trying to understand the dominant philosophy. It holds that experience is basically sense perception. Accordingly, the nonhuman world is the world known in sense perception—that is, a world of sense data. Sense data have no significant reality apart from being perceived. Given this starting point, the only role that things-in-themselves could play would be as causes of human experience of the sense data. But that does not work either. When we begin with sense perception we can only understand cause and effect as a relation between sense data. There is no way of moving from sense perception to significant things-in-themselves.

The dominant philosophy leads to some paradoxical consequences that it usually fails to acknowledge. These can be vividly seen in terms of the evolutionary view of the rise of the human species. This view is scientifically well established and almost never questioned by philosophers. But human development out of lower forms of life is difficult for the dominant philosophy to incorporate. For strict consistency this philosophy would have to assert one of two things. Either the whole of reality came into being abruptly out of nothing with the advent of human beings; or a totally unknowable and insignificant reality was transformed radically into a human one at this point.

It will be sufficient to explain the first of these alternatives. According to the dominant philosophy the only reality of which we can usefully speak is human experience and its perceived objects. We cannot speak of what these perceived objects are in themselves. Hence, before humans appeared there was no reality of which we can speak. Only when human experience began could there be the objects of human experience—sun and moon, wolves and cattle, sticks and stones—whether these are conceived as sense data or as perceived objects.

This is obviously a very strange doctrine. It would mean that all the events that produced the planet and started the evolutionary development that culminated in us became real abruptly, either when we emerged or when we first learned about them. But the whole thrust of evolutionary theory is just the opposite. It teaches that there were billions of years of real occurrences, that we appeared very late, and that no sharp line separated us from our animal ancestors. Surely our philosophy should take account of this scientific view of our place in the world!

Few philosophers of the dominant tradition intend these paradoxical consequences of their anthropocentric view of reality. Hence, when pressed, they will make concessions. For example, they will sometimes acknowledge that the higher animals have experiences too. They may even extend experience to all animals equipped with sense organs.

But the problems of the dominant philosophy cannot be solved by concessions. We are no better off if we think of reality as coming into being abruptly out of nothing with the advent of the first organ of vision, or hearing, or touch. According to all the evidence, the sense organs, too, developed gradually at the end of a long evolutionary process.

For philosophy to take serious account of evolution would require it to transform itself radically. It must find a way of attributing to the world out of which animal and human experience arose a reality that is continuous with that of human experience. That is not easy to do. It is impossible as long as human experience is understood basically as sense perception. Obviously there was nothing like sense perception until there were such things as sense organs.

In recent times Teilhard de Chardin has provided an influential expression of evolutionary philosophy. He has helped us to think of experience as consciousness, or as the "within" of things. He taught that all things have both this "within" as well as the "without" that the dominant philosophy has had in view.

We can think of the "within" of things as what things are in themselves. We can then understand that the only way in which things can be viewed as having significant reality in themselves is to see them as having reality also *for them-selves*.

This point is crucial. The dominant philosophy has been undecided as to whether to allow that nonhuman things have some reality in themselves. But it has consistently assumed that if they have such reality, it is of no significance. That is because the idea of something in itself, apart from any experience whatever, really is an empty idea. If we are to attribute significant reality to something apart from our experience, it must be in terms of some other experience. When we deal with other human beings, we assume that they continue to have their experiences even when we do not experience them. They are seeing trees and buildings and other people even when we do not see them. That is why their reality and value do not depend on their reality and value for us. They exist *in* themselves as something *for* themselves. But the dominant philosophy has been reluctant to admit that nonhuman things are something *for* themselves as well.

An evolutionary philosophy must affirm that what existed before human beings, and before the sensory experience of animals, was already something for itself. The emergence of humans and the much earlier emergence of sensory experience can still be regarded as very important events. But they can then be viewed as parts of a continuous development rather that abrupt creations out of nothing.

The acknowledgment of the reality of nonhuman things for themselves cannot be treated as a minor concession within the dominant philosophy. Its implications contradict the fundamental assumptions of that philosophy. The nature of experience, of relatedness, of subject and object, and of cause and effect must all be fundamentally reconceived.

Teilhard pointed toward the philosophical reconstruction that is needed, but he did not carry it through. Fortunately, this has been done by Alfred North Whitehead. Whitehead developed his philosophy not with evolutionary problems alone in view, but in close relation also to quantum mechanics and relativity theory, as well as to theoretical issues in twentieth-century logic and mathematics. The resulting vision is the one we need. But it is not easy to understand or appropriate. The next chapter offers an introduction.

Whitehead: An Ecological Philosophy

In philosophy a great deal depends on the examples used. In explaining the dominant philosophy I used "seeing-a-chair" as the instance of experience to be analyzed. The dominant philosophy takes that kind of experience as basic. It understands other forms of experience, such as awareness of the functioning of one's body, experience of other people, thinking, emotional feeling, memory, and anticipation, as either analogous to the seeing of a chair or as analyzable into elements that are like it. We have already followed the inevitable consequences of this starting point.

In the previous chapter we noted that if we are to make any sense of evolution we must understand experience in some other way. Conscious sense perception must be seen to have developed gradually out of some more primitive form of experience. Whitehead points out that we know physiologically, too, that conscious sense perception is the product of complex events. There is no reason to suppose that it is a simple and primary form of experience, or that all other aspects of experience must be explained by it. We are well advised to seek more fundamental aspects of experience even if they are outside of clear consciousness.

Instead of analyzing seeing-a-chair, let us consider experiencing-in-the-present-moment-the-feeling-of-pleasure-one-had-a-moment-ago. Usually this is felt as simply continuing to enjoy that pleasure. But it is not as simple as that. Continuation through time requires renewal in each moment. And sometimes experience of the past feeling is not simply its continuation. For example, I might now feel ashamed at having felt pleasure in someone else's misfortune.

The dominant philosophy, if it would pay attention to this kind of example at all, would try to explain it on the analogy of sense perception. Sense perception does not relate us to its object as something for itself. Hence, the dominant philosophy would analyze this feeling of a past feeling as if the past feeling were a mere object for the new subject. It views the past feeling as analogous to a visual object.

Whitehead, however, turns the tables. For him, the feeling of feeling is primary. He explains in detail how clear and distinct conscious sense perceptions arise out of myriads of these far more elementary experiences. For example, the transmission of nerve impulses from cell to cell, which makes possible visual and auditory perceptions of the external world, can be analyzed into unconscious feelings of the feelings in the eye and ear and through the nerves. The final unification and projection of visual and auditory data is based on a unified human feeling of the many feelings of the cells in the brain. In the higher phases of this synthesis consciousness emerges.

The problem with the dominant philosophy is much like that with Newtonian science, which is not surprising since the two developed together. The dominant philosophy tries to understand all experience as being like ordinary sense perception. The Newtonian science tried to understand all objects as being like the objects of ordinary sense perception. Newtonian science broke down when it became clear that the ingredients which made up objects like chairs were not at all like little bits of cloth or wood, but were instead events or processes. Scientists went on to the study of electromagnetic events. But philosophers of the dominant school continued to think about the kind of reality possessed by chairs. Since it is quite implausible to think of a chair as something for itself, they quite properly continued to deny that any significant reality could be attributed to it in itself.

If, however, we turn our attention away from chairs to the electromagnetic events that make them up, the situation changes. Most of what we mean by a chair has no reality apart from its perception and use by us. Electromagnetic events were occurring for a long time before there were human beings, or even animals, around. They must have had their reality in themselves, and that makes sense only if we also affirm that they had reality for themselves. To have reality for itself an entity must feel. Since feeling is the most primitive form of "taking account of," and since there is excellent evidence that electromagnetic events do take account of their environment, it is reasonable to affirm that they are instances of unconscious feeling.

It is useful to recognize that reality, value, and kinship extend in this tenuous way to the most elementary particles that make up our world, but our major concern is with living things. No sharp line divides the animate from the inanimate. The features we associate with life came into being gradually at the end of a long development. Our concern for the animate must shade off into concern for the total process and the whole of reality. But it is the animate, and especially the higher forms of life, that are now threatened with extinction. It is toward these that we need to extend our sense of kinship and concern. We are fellow creatures of an age-long creative process, sharing a common history and perhaps a common destiny.

Whitehead explains that an event is alive to the extent that it includes novelty. All events repeat elements from their past. But in some events new elements appear, elements added in the event itself. This novelty may be trivial or important. The event may be more or less alive.

The things we ordinarily call alive are not individual events but vast societies of events, such as a mouse or a tree. These societies are alive to whatever extent there are events among their members whose life affects the social organization as a whole.

Along with the novel response goes a heightening of feeling. A living event takes account of much more of its world, with far greater intensity, than does an inorganic event. The inorganic event achieves its unity by simple repetition of simple feelings. That requires the screening out of most of the complexity and intensity of feelings offered it by its world. A living event can take account of much more of its world because it achieves its unity by its own creative response.

It is this greater richness of feeling and the ever new potentialities of living processes that can elicit our proper reverence.

Whitehead's philosophy pictures for us a world filled with real events, each having its own intrinsic value. Especially those that are alive significantly share with us in feeling and activity. It is therein that the needed attitude of love, concern, or reverence for living things is adequately and rationally grounded.

This philosophy also describes these real and valuable events as interrelated and interconnected in just the way that is implied by the ecological attitude. We ignore this at our peril. As Whitehead says in *Science and the Modern World,* "The two evils are: one, the ignoration of the true relation of each organism and the environment; and the other, the habit of ignoring the intrinsic worth of the environment which must be allowed its weight in any consideration of final ends."[1]

The environment of which Whitehead speaks is composed not of substances but of events. These do not first exist and then have things happen to them. They come into being only in the process of taking account of other events.

Consider, again, a moment of human experience as an event. That momentary experience comes into being and then passes away. It grows out of the preceding moment of human experience. It also takes account of what is going on in the body and in the wider environment. It does not first exist as something else and then take account of these things. It comes into being as a process of taking account of these other events. Without them it would not be what it is. They give it its content.

What is true of a human experience is true of all events. Each comes into being as a process of taking account of other events. It has no other being or reality. It is not identical with the events it feels. Its reality for itself is unique and irreducible. But it is not independent. It exists only as a synthesis of its world.

Just as each event comes into being as a taking account of its world, so every event becomes a part of the world of which subsequent events must take account. The consequences of each event spread out in complex ways through the entire future, interacting with the consequences of all the other events. The whole universe is one vast ecological system. Both the events that make up the human personality and those that constitute the cells in the human body belong to that system.

There is still another way in which the environment enters into a person and constitutes him or her. Seeing a landscape or a painting is not an incidental occurrence that leaves a person fundamentally unaffected. On the contrary, the beauty of nature or art shares in constituting his or her very being. Whitehead shows us that the beauty of the environment "adds to the permanent richness of the soul's self-attainment."[2]

It is clear that the ordinary ways of separating history from nature, or human beings from other creatures, are undercut in Whitehead's vision. In conclusion, it will be useful to note one final way in which Whitehead frees us from this dualism.

In the Newtonian age people were impressed by natural law as something

immutably binding physical things. In humans they found a freedom that tran-
scended such law. This freedom, they thought, distinguished humanity and human
history from law-bound nature.

In this respect, too, the Newtonian vision has broken down in science, but it
retains considerable power in philosophy and in the general vision of reality out
of which people operate. However, in Whitehead's view, even the laws of nature
are not immutable. There are innumerable events each taking account of its world
in its own way. The individual events constitute themselves in some measure
unpredictably, but for the most part they reenact dominant elements in their past.
When we are dealing with vast numbers of them, and in the physical sciences we
usually are, the indeterminateness of the behavior of each individual is unimpor-
tant. The behavior of the aggregate can be predicted within narrow limits and with
high probability. We can formulate these predictive descriptions in "laws." But if
so, then laws are a function of the behavior of real things in the world. They do not
determine that behavior. The behavior determines them and the behavior can
change. With the emergence of new societies new laws emerge.

The emergence of new laws is most apparent in the historical process. The laws
describing the average behavior of contemporary Americans in sexual relations
did not exist before contemporary Americans existed. They will change gradually
as the behavior of individual Americans changes. Most of the laws of the social
sciences are of this sort.

Laws about the behavior of biological species are similar. These laws come into
being with the evolutionary emergence of the species, change with its evolutionary
development, and cease to operate if the species is exterminated. The laws about
homing pigeons depend upon the behavior of individual homing pigeons. If new
behavior patterns are developed by breeding, the laws will change.

Of course, human beings differ from each other much more than animals of a
single species differ. Human culture changes much more rapidly than animal
behavior patterns. The difference is very great and very important. These and
other differences can and should be described in detail. This description can be
carried through in the categories of Whitehead's philosophy. The differences
should be stressed and affirmed as the objective justification for our peculiar
concentration of concern on our own survival and welfare. But they are differences within a single world, whether we call it nature, or history, or an ecological
system. They do not make us outsiders. They do not reduce the other products of
the creative evolutionary process to mere objects without intrinsic value. There is
no dualism of humanity and its environment.

The Commitment We Need

For traditional Christianity, the transcendent creator alone is sacred. Humanity and the rest of the world are jointly God's creation. As created they have value derived from their creator. From this agreed point, there can be two lines of development. It is possible, on the one side, to stress that all God's creatures are valuable to God and, hence, in themselves. In this case it is natural and proper to emphasize our co-creaturehood with all and to extend love to all. But on the other side, Christianity teaches that we alone are made in the image of God and that God has established humanity as lord over all other creatures. It sometimes so accentuates our supreme and unique importance that all other things become mere means to our ends. This tendency has dominated Western Christendom. Even here, however, some sense of stewardship is encouraged. Humanity may be lord of all other creatures, but it is accountable to a far superior lord, the creator of all.

Traditional Christianity is still an important force, but for several centuries its influence in the West has been declining. Its major successor has been humanism. Some forms of humanism have stressed their continuity with Christianity; others have emphasized their opposition. Whether or not belief in God is retained by humanists, they shift the real locus of the sacred to human beings. In this way, the process of separating humans from their fellow creatures, already begun in traditional Christianity, is completed. Other living things have no significant reality or value except in relation to humanity. They belong to human beings, who owe no accounting to anyone except themselves for how they use them. Concern for these creatures as they are in themselves would be pure sentimentality. Animals, for example, exist for the humanist only as pets, sources of energy, livestock, game, pests, specimens, or occasionally, aesthetic objects.

Humanism is today the most unifying form of faith. Traditional religions tend to emphasize their humanistic elements in order to be relevant in our time. Humanism is expressed in the charter of the United Nations and guides the more enlightened leaders in the developing nations. But, like traditional Christianity, humanism is declining. The reason for the decline has little to do with its attitude toward animals. The reason is its inherent instability.

Humanism thrives on attacking otherworldly and superstitious elements in traditional religion and culture. Against them it calls for the affirmation of present human values and the application of critical reason to the solution of human problems. But it has no new basis or ground for its affirmation of humanity. It derives its vision of the sacredness of human personality from the traditional Christianity it rejects.

Indeed, it is difficult for humanism to state clearly where its commitment lies. Is there a sacred essence of humanity in which all people participate? Or is the object of commitment the sum total of all individual human beings now alive? Is it human personality as it actually exists that is sacred? Or are we to commit ourselves to the realization of a potential that has not yet been actualized?

Important practical consequences follow from the answers to these questions. Some answers indicate that the unlimited multiplication of human life is desirable, regardless of the problems which that creates. Other answers indicate that the realization of the human essence or potential is far more important than the multiplication of individuals. But no matter how the questions are answered, serious difficulties arise. The critical rationality that humanists have directed against traditional religions plays havoc with humanism as well. Its arbitrary elements become more and more apparent, and as this occurs, its power to elicit commitment declines.

The operation of critical reason on humanist pretensions leads to secular atheism. For secular atheism nothing is sacred, or ultimate, or absolute. Hence, there are no *basic* commitments, only provisional ones. Everything is seen as means to ends which are themselves judged by their contributions to further ends. All belief in the sacred is perceived as a threat to the needed pragmatic rationality. Strong people can recognize the relativity of all values. They do not need to believe that actions have *ultimate* importance in order to take them. They can establish their own norms and live effectively by them without the illusion that they have a higher sanction. Indeed, by removing all such sanctions, they believe that they can have greater freedom and greater tolerance of the freedom of others. Even if there is some pain in the loss of the sacred, they prefer to live freely and without illusion rather than to submit again to authority.

Secular atheism has two conflicting tendencies in relation to the nonhuman world. On the one hand, since it denies the sacredness of human personality, it deflates human pretensions to distinctiveness and thinks of human beings as much more like the other animals. On the other hand, it subscribes to the thoroughly anthropocentric philosophies of empiricism and positivism. Furthermore, the recognition of kinship between humans and the other animals tends rather to disparage the worth of humans than to encourage concern for other living things. Secular atheism is closely associated with the technological attitude and tends to apply it even to the treatment of human beings.

Humanism gains its power by freeing us from the shackles of superstition and displays its weakness when required to stand on its own feet. Similarly, secular atheism gains its power by its clear-sighted critique of both traditional religion and humanism and finds that it has little to offer in itself. On many university campuses it no longer plays the role of rebel; for it is now established as academic orthodoxy. At this point its barrenness and emptiness become apparent. It has little to say on the important issues of life. It hides its nakedness in specializations of questionable usefulness. It claims freedom from all absolutes, but it has no ends toward which to use its freedom. It turns away from the interior life and treats all things, including human beings, as objects. The objectivity it achieves belongs to death rather than life.

At least these are the criticisms directed against secular atheism by many of the youth who come into contact with it. Largely in reaction to it, there is arising now a fresh and vital paganism. People are rediscovering the sacred in the dance, in communal intimacy, and in the mysteries of bodily feeling. The popular musical *Hair* celebrates this new tribalism with evangelical fervor. The new pagans are irreverent toward the traditional Christian and humanistic symbols of the sacred. They are not concerned with displaying the sacred as either unified or transcendent. They are satisfied in the immediacy of the experience of the sacred power. They call on us to regain the lost awareness of the sacred in all the varied experiences of life. Then we will stop treating these experiences as pragmatic means to some future or transcendent good and enjoy them as ends in themselves. Not theories about the universe, but the concentration of energy and feeling in the now is the proper expression of this renewal of religious experience.

In general the new paganism, like the old, is far more in tune with the vitalities and rhythms of nature than are traditional Christianity, humanism, and secular atheism. The sacred is found not only in human community and bodily ecstasy but in the natural environment as well. The healing of human individuals and society is regarded as requiring a new balance and harmony with the nonhuman world. People must find themselves in and with the natural processes rather than outside and against them. Those human feelings that rise directly out of the organism are trusted more than those that have been culturally molded.

The new paganism has a much more affirmative message than the atheistic secularism with which it vies on the university scene. But it, too, has its weaknesses. It, too, is more powerful in its protest against the aridity of the dominant atheism than in its own independent affirmations. The secular atheist rightly points out that these affirmations cannot be taken quite seriously in the adult world. The critical faculty is too well established in our culture. It can be set aside for short periods of recreation or celebration, but we cannot ignore the fact that our actions have consequences that we need to consider before we act. The blind quest for an immediacy in which to lose self-awareness is humanly destructive. We should at least use rational criteria in deciding which gods to worship. But when we examine what the new paganism finds to be sacred, it often appears as nothing more than certain types of experience that can be induced in controlled ways. As such, they lose their sacredness and become just one more part of the secular world. The blind quest for community is not only escapist but dangerous. Communities can be competitive and mutually destructive. When they are viewed as sacred, the possibility of criticizing their actions, and thereby gaining independence from them, is lost. A new tribalism is the last thing we need on a crowded planet. It would prove divisive rather than unifying. It can provide no responsible guidance for the vast industrial and economic changes that must occur if we are to survive the ecological crisis.

There is truth in the criticisms directed by each of these movements against the other. Thus far the degree of truth has been partly obscured by the remaining power of humanism within them. Those who think they reject the sacred entirely sometimes continue to assume the peculiar importance and worth of human beings in a way their own principles do not justify. In this way they are saved from the worst consequences of their atheism. Likewise, the new paganism is still far more humanistic than the old. Thus a principle of self-criticism is present that still functions effectively from time to time. But we cannot assume that humanistic habits will last indefinitely. As they are outgrown, the inherent weaknesses of both movements will be increasingly obvious.

Neither secular atheism nor the new paganism provides the focus for a long-term commitment to the healing of our natural environment. Secular atheism is involved in the technological attitude. It is suited to the efficient achievement of arbitrary ends. The ends are usually set by a society that is still largely humanistic or nationalistic. The new paganism has recovered a sense of unity with the environment and respect for it, but in the commitment to immediacy it has abandoned the critical reflection apart from which we cannot cope with our ecological problems.

We cannot return to humanism even though it continues to be pervasively influential. Its internal instability is now too obvious. In any case, its separation of humanity from nature is just what we do not want. We need a new, inclusive commitment that will direct our concern to the nonhuman world as well as to humanity and that will guide and sustain intelligent action through thick and thin.

An apparent solution would be to view all nature, or at least all life, as sacred. Thereby we would achieve the goal of inclusiveness. But in other respects this would be calamitous. There is truth, if only a very one-sided truth, in the bitter poem by Matthew Arnold ironically entitled "In Harmony with Nature."

> Know, man hath all which Nature hath, but more,
> And in that *more* lie all his hopes of good.
> Nature is cruel, man is sick of blood;
> Nature is stubborn, man would fain adore;
> Nature is fickle, man hath need of rest;
> Nature forgives no debt, and fears no grave;
> Man would be mild, and with safe conscience blest.
> Man must begin, know this, where Nature ends;
> Nature and man can never be fast friends.
> Fool, if thou canst not pass her, rest her slave![1]

These lines express much that has proved destructive in the Western vision of humanity and nature. Their spirit must be profoundly rejected if we are to respond adequately to our present crisis. But Arnold's point cannot be ignored. As Whitehead pointed out, life is robbery. Life preys on life. In the quest to sustain their own lives and to perpetuate their species, animals are ruthless in the destruction of other life, plant or animal. We, too, must participate in this process of destruction, but we should not make it the object of our commitment.

The concern we need to extend to all things is better symbolized by stewardship than by commitment. To commit ourselves either to individual living things or to the sum total of all would inhibit responsible stewardship rather than promote it. Stewardship must be governed not only by respect for the goodness things embody but also by a vision of the good that is yet to be realized.

Yet stewardship is not an adequate concept either. Although it suggests that humanity is an outsider, humanity is a part of that for which it is concerned and responsible. Although stewardship suggests that humanity brings adequate knowledge with it to its task and can control what occurs, it must learn from the world for which it cares how to serve and work with it.

The better image is of a participant in a process of healing and growth. Such participants have responsibilities, but they are not the masters. There is something going on that they do not manage, something that they must learn to adjust to and work with. Since we are ourselves part of nature, we can recognize that process working in ourselves, both in our bodies and in our personalities, as well as in our environment. We can develop sensitivity to that process and by restraint and openness assist its working both within and without.

The process which we cannot manipulate, but whose working we can facilitate, must be discriminated from the totality of events in the universe. It is not expressed in hurricanes, or earthquakes, or the force of gravity, although these, too, are parts of nature. It is the process that makes for life and the enrichment of life, variety of forms, intensity of experience, consciousness, and love.

But this process is not identical with the individual things that it has produced. Toward the individual things love or concern is the attitude we need. But toward the process that gives them life and enriches life another attitude is appropriate. To it we can commit ourselves. This commitment need not be hesitant, provisional, or tentative. It can and should be basic. If this process is what we mean by "nature" or "life," then we can and should view "nature" or "life" as sacred. But it will be better to speak of it as Creative Process or as God.

To commit ourselves to God, understood in this way, would be to seek to promote life in its variety and intensity as well as in its consciousness and love. It would encourage reflective inquiry and selective appraisal of the relation of means and ends. But it would also encourage sensitivity, passion, and community. It would provide a critical norm by which to evaluate the many claimants to loyalty and service. It would undergird our commitment to a healthy balance of human and nonhuman life and would keep us sensitive to the total ecological consequences of our acts. It would encourage and even require just that extension of love to the nonhuman world that is the hallmark of the new Christianity.

Is Commitment Possible?

Many will agree that to commit ourselves to the process that creates and sustains life, variety, intensity, consciousness, and love would be useful and beneficial. But is such commitment possible?

If commitment were something entirely voluntary, this question would not arise. Provisional commitments are like that. In order to work for peace, one is quite free to commit oneself provisionally to campaigning for a peace candidate. One has only to choose. But here it is a matter of *basic* commitment. Our basic commitments arise in response to our sense of something that is *absolutely* important or good, something sacred. They arise as we are "grasped" by something rather than through choice.

If that were the whole story, however, there would be no point in discussing basic commitments at all. They would just happen at random. Actually the relation between choosing and being chosen is more complicated than that. Even our basic commitments are subject to erosion through critical reflection, as the histories of Christianity and humanism show. Similarly, as a new way of looking at the world arises, new features take on importance. One can train oneself to view matters in a new light and even to act in new ways. Even *basic* commitments are partly shaped in this way.

Still it remains true that basic commitments emerge and are not simply chosen. It would be useless to call for a basic commitment to something whose absolute importance and goodness could not be made apparent, and thereby grasp the human spirit. Hence, one cannot sensibly call for commitment to something that on closer inspection appears unworthy or unreal.

The question must be asked here: Is the process that produces life, variety, intensity, consciousness, and love such that, as we examine it more closely, our sense of its importance and worth is enhanced? Or is the reverse the case?

Suppose that on examination we found the phrase misleading. It implies that there is some significant unity since we can talk of "*the* process." Perhaps on examination we would find that the process that produces life and the process that produces love are quite distinct and even incompatible. Then the call for commitment in its present form would be meaningless. At best, one would have to choose between the process that makes for life and the one that makes for love.

Or suppose that on examination we decided that there is no single factor or process that makes for life. Perhaps there are only myriads of blind happenings which from time to time in varied and unpredictable ways produce or sustain life. Then again the call to commitment would be meaningless.

I am convinced that examination of the process does not lead to either of these conclusions, that one and the same factor in the universe functions to produce and sustain life wherever it occurs and encourages in us the widest extension of concern to other living beings. But all such affirmations about reality confront much doubt and incredulity. They involve beliefs about the world that do not fit comfortably with the intellectual habits of our time. For that reason, these beliefs seem implausible or irrelevant. Further, the ordinary idea of a process or a factor in the universe is so vague, that it is useless to call for commitment to it and meaningless to call it God.

The major reason for the decline of belief in God in the modern world is that this belief has seemed increasingly out of step with the rest of modern thought. Part of the awkwardness stemmed from scientific discoveries. The ordinary presentation of belief in God implied things that did not correspond with reliable scientific theory. Certainly this weakened the credibility of theism. But this was not the basic problem. Theism could be modified, and was modified, to fit the facts as they became known. Part of the difficulty came from the authoritarian way the doctrine was presented and the authoritarian cast given to the belief itself. Certainly this alienated many of the most creative and sensitive moderns. But this was not the basic problem either. Theism could be presented in a fully liberal spirit, and it often was. The basic problem was that it could not be successfully modified to fit the vision of reality expressed in the dominant philosophy.

The dominant philosophy has declared human experience to be the measure of all things. "Man is the measure" not only of value or importance, but also of reality or being. Dogs and chairs have no reality except as they function in human experience. The same is true of God. From the point of view of the dominant philosophy, the reality of God can only be God's reality for us.

To think of the process that produces life and has produced it through millions of years as having its reality only for us is a very confusing idea. We try to picture the process as it appears to us, and we fail. Hence, the notion of such a process cannot grasp our imagination, and the process itself cannot evoke our commitment. Unless the process is fully real in itself, and unless we can seriously think of it as such, the needed commitment cannot arise. This is the crux of the problem.

Theologians have sometimes made a virtue of this situation. We know nothing, they declare, of what God is in-and-for God. In any case, it would be a merely conceptual knowledge, and the attempt to gain it would be an expression of lack of faith. They warn that when we try to think about God as such, we put *our* concepts in place of the living God or reduce God to a creature of our minds. According to these theologians, our only concern should be what God is for us. And what God is for us is what is revealed in Jesus Christ. In Christ, they say, we have saving knowledge of God, and this is the only knowledge of God that God grants us.

Now this view, held by many of the leading Protestant theologians of the last generation, is not to be lightly dismissed. Certainly it is more important to know how God deals with us than to know something about God that is irrelevant to us. Yet the position must be rejected. It does not work. There are good logical reasons why it does not work, and the actual results in our generation have borne out these reasons. This view of the relation of God to us as given *only* in Christ has led with perfect consistency to the atheistic Christianity of our time. The leaders of that movement were brought up on the view I have been describing. It did not work for them. Let me explain.

When one said in those days that God is known only in Jesus Christ, one still assumed that the word *God* in the sentence meant something. One did not mean to say simply that Jesus Christ is known only in Jesus Christ. That would not have been very interesting. One meant that some kind of transcendent and even omnipotent reality made itself known in Jesus Christ. But what is presupposed in the sentence is then denied by it too. To have a notion of something transcendent and omnipotent and to bring that notion with you to be reshaped by Jesus Christ is one thing. To have no notion at all and to come blankly to Jesus Christ is another. If one does the former, one does not know God only in Jesus Christ, although in one's encounter with Jesus one may discover how inadequate and even false was one's earlier notion of God. If one does the latter, one will have no more reason to speak of God after meeting Jesus than before. In meeting Jesus one will have met *only* Jesus. If someone tells one that Jesus is sometimes called God, it will mean nothing more than if some other proper name is given him. If God is known only in Jesus Christ, then God quite simply must be Jesus Christ, and nothing is gained by using this additional name.

Of course, no one has ever really meant that, or more accurately, those who do mean that have stopped talking about God. The theologians of the last generation talked a great deal about God and said many things about God they would not have said about Jesus. But they used this doctrine to forbid raising the question as to what the word *God* means. They spoke as if *God* pointed to some reality that was objectively real to and for man, but they turned attention away from the question as to whether that was the case and, if so, how it could be the case. Those were philosophical questions, and they opposed the intrusion of philosophy into theology.

If we now try to speak of God, again we face the philosophical problem behind this theological position. The dominant philosophy only allows us to speak of God as God is for us just as it only allows us to speak of dogs and pencils as they are for us. The dominant philosophy, however, introduces an additional difficulty in speaking of God. Since we can see and touch dogs and pencils, even if they have no reality for themselves, they do have indubitable reality for us. But God does not appear in sense experience.

That God does not appear in sense experience has been a basic part of the whole biblical-Christian tradition. But it has not led to disbelief because it has been accompanied by two other beliefs: God is at least sometimes experienced nonsensuously; and what is experienced through the senses or otherwise gives evidence of God's reality. However, the dominant philosophy has made difficulties for both of these doctrines.

The dominant philosophy may admit that there are some nonsensuous feelings, such as the feeling of the holy, that are associated with belief in God. But such experience must be understood as analogous to sense experience. The holy we experience is nothing other than a part of our experience. Furthermore, in this perspective, whereas the pencil and dog do not belong only to my private experience but also to that of many other people, my experience of the holy is quite simply my own. Such purely private experiences are generally disparaged. And even if they are fully admitted, we are left only with a bit of private experience. To call that God would be odd indeed.

Primarily, Christians have assumed that the events of history and nature as well as private experience have given them warrant to speak of a reality that is not identical with those events. The way one reasons from what is given to something not given is by arguing from an effect to its cause. But in the dominant philosophy, one cannot reason from the world or any aspect of it to God as its cause. On its principles the cause, like the effect, must belong to the contents of experience. Perhaps a feeling of the holy might be the cause of worship. But in these terms God cannot be the cause of anything. If God is not the cause of anything, there is no reason to suppose that God exists or that, if God did exist, it would make any difference.

Whitehead, we saw, holds to quite different principles. Experience is basically and primarily nonsensory. It begins with the feeling of our past and of our bodies. What is felt is experienced as having had its own reality in and for itself. That this is so is evidenced in aspects of our surest and most pervasive beliefs, but it is not clearly given in vivid consciousness. We reason from clear consciousness to what must have been in order that this consciousness be as it is. Our consciousness is an effect of causes.

There is no proof here of the reality of God, but the question is entirely open. No special pleading, leap of faith, or appeal to dogma is required. Along with our dim but pervasive experience of our past feelings, of our bodies, and of our environing world, is there also an experience of a creative process? If so, there is reason to affirm God as real, just as the past experiences, the body, and the environing world are real in and for themselves. Whitehead believes that the order and especially the novelty that characterize every experience, as well as the aim of each experience to fulfill some relevant possibility, bear witness that a creative influence is effective in every event. He sees evidence also in the special intuitions and experiences of the world's great religious figures. Most followers of Whitehead have agreed that there are reasons to speak of God.

I have been sketching how the same doctrines that have concealed from us the autonomous reality and value of the nonhuman world also excluded the possibility of believing in God. The same philosophical reform that opens up the possibility of affirming unabashedly the autonomous reality of the nonhuman world also reopens the question of God. Hence the discussion of God's reality should begin. In *this* context it makes sense.

For the discussion to begin afresh, it should be really open not only with respect to God's reality but also with respect to what God is like. A God who plays a discernible role in every experience and every event is a very different God than one likened to a watchmaker who observes the results of "His" handiwork from a distance. This God differs also from the supernatural deity who intervenes from time to time to benefit "His" favorites. A God who is affected by all that happens, suffering in all suffering and rejoicing in all rejoicing, is very different from the impassive deity of an earlier orthodoxy. And a God who always persuades and never coerces or compels is very different from the omnipotent sovereign to whose will all must resign themselves.

The difference is indeed great, so great that some have suggested that the old word God should be abandoned if our evidence points, as Whitehead thought, to this kind of a reality. Perhaps we should speak only of Life, of Nature, or of Creative Process. Perhaps we should speak of the Word or of Christ, since the everywhere active, suffering, persuading, life-giving reality who emerges from Whitehead's analysis is recognized by him as manifest in a peculiar way in Jesus.

I am not ready to make this change in terminology. It is my hope that we can rescue the word *God* from the oppressive and repressive and unreal connotations it has come to have for so many people. Perhaps we can give it new meaning, at once more Christian and more universal, at once more personal and more natural. But if this is what we are to do, we must not think in terms of recovering old beliefs about God but about discovering God afresh. Of course, there will be elements of recovery. Every new growth must have its roots in the past. If there were no continuity, it would be wrong to speak of God at all. But the vision we need of nature and of our place in it cannot develop by repeating a past view, whether biblical or traditional. It will reflect and be shaped by that history. But it must grow out of reflection on ecology, evolution, human biology, and contemporary philosophy as well. Likewise, a view of God to be viable in our time must develop in intimate relation with all that we know of the universe and its total history, and of the human role within it. It will not do to take a received idea and adapt it only under the pressure of necessity when its falsity and irrelevance are forced on our attention. Our view of God must not be a reluctant compromise with science and modernity. It must be fully rooted in our present situation, fully affirming what the evidence suggests.

I do not mean that we should believe only what a majority of intellectuals of our time believe. The majority have rarely been right. In any case, when I speak of finding God afresh in our time I am speaking as a Christian. Christians are those who have been shaped in their perception of meaning and importance and in the very structure of their existence by Jesus. What we as Christians seek when we seek God in our time is not sought by all. Our questions are not the same as those that have been formed by the dominant philosophy. We are driven by concerns that do not drive everyone. The God we seek is the Christian God, but what we today find as the Christian God may differ profoundly from the God of Augustine, of Thomas, of Calvin, of Schleiermacher, or of Barth.

For example, if we now use the language of creation, we will not be referring to some one act of God thousands or billions of years ago. We will not be speaking of the once-for-all ordaining of supposed immutable laws of nature. Such a view may have made sense in the Newtonian age, but it makes none in ours. It could have importance only if it were supposed that God would intervene in God's creation from without to save us from the consequences of our actions. But to believe that is to undercut human responsibility and to run counter to ages of human experience and spiritual maturation.

The creative action of God which concerns us is the creation that takes place now, moment by moment, in our environment and in ourselves. In each moment God confronts the totality of the past with new possibilities. How the world responds, whether in acceptance or rejection of these possibilities, God does not determine. God creates by persuasion in and through the free decisions of the creatures. To believe in God is to trust this creative work amongst and within us, to adapt ourselves to it, to attend to it as it operates in all creatures, to sensitize ourselves to it as it works in us, and to respond to its call to new risks.

Belief in God is thus not only a part of a total vision within which science and technology can become servants of life rather than conquerors of nature. It is also the basis of the kind of response to the present crisis apart from which this crisis may be humanity's last.

Is It Too Late?

There are many consequences that follow from what has been said. Artists, writers, journalists, philosophers, and scientists need to work together with politicians, economists, technicians, and naturalists to form the new consciousness that we need and to work out its implications for personal conduct, social order, and international relations. A task of special importance and magnitude falls upon the churches. Despite their loss of power and prestige, they remain the major religious institutions of our society and the bearers of a great heritage. If the vision and life we now need is a new, more naturalistic Christianity, and not primitivism, or Taoism, or paganism, or secular humanism, then the church is particularly challenged to carry through its own transformation and to give leadership in the shaping of this new vision of reality. Vision and commitment are formed above all in worship. In the quest for new and more relevant forms of worship, the churches must take great care as to what is communicated through these new forms. They have in their hands instruments of enormous power. Let them take care how they use these instruments.

The church has another task as well—to promote the needed spirit of personal and national sacrifice for the larger and the longer good. This has been central to Christian self-understanding throughout the centuries. The cross of Jesus Christ is the focus of our faith, and we know that we are called on to take up our own crosses. In recent years the call to sacrifice has often been muted. We have heard more about self-fulfillment and self-realization than about self-denial. But the time has come to return to this more basic theme of Christian tradition. For the sake of future generations, our generation is called upon to repent of its self-indulgent ways, to discipline itself, and to accept reductions in the standard of living to which it has grown so quickly accustomed. As individuals we are called upon to give up goals we have long sought and the leisure and relaxation we so enjoy in order to take actions that antagonize our erstwhile friends.

Activists may grow impatient with all this talk. To them it seems that new knowledge and new laws—not a new vision, or consciousness, or spirit—are all we need. If we stand on the brink of catastrophe, if decisions that will be made tomorrow will settle our fate, then is not all this talk of changes in our basic attitudes, changes that will certainly require years, irrelevant and distracting? Above all, should we not give up talking about God and concentrate instead on the tasks ahead? These are serious questions, and they should be seriously regarded. Is it, perhaps, already too late?

Certainly the projection of present trends for even two or three decades is frightening. The rate of growth of world population is likely to increase. New grains will temporarily ease the problem of food shortages, but they will heighten our dependence on a few crops. Crop failures will have increasingly disastrous results over wider areas. The percentage of the world population whose brains have been permanently damaged by lack of proteins in childhood will increase. The urgency of finding new sources of food will lead to the decimation of the most edible types of ocean fish. Under the pressure to produce food, more forests will be cut down and marginal land brought under cultivation. The permanent loss of topsoils will be accelerated. Meanwhile, the use of agricultural chemicals will increase, poisoning streams and lakes and killing birds. Poisons will continue to find their way up the food chain to the human body. Wild animals above the size of small rodents will disappear outside of zoos. These rodents, like insects, will become increasingly difficult to control as their natural enemies are exterminated. We will resort to wholesale poisoning with further damage to the environment.

Pollution of the oceans will increase rapidly. Large portions will be covered by oil. The coral islands will disintegrate. The coastal areas will be poisoned, and all the varieties of marine life dependent on them will disappear. If plankton are decimated, the results will be still more horrendous, for plankton are the basis of the food chain in the ocean.

A blanket of smog will cover the planet, reducing agricultural output and shortening human life. Local conditions will vary. Temporary concentrations of smog will kill thousands of people in cities, and life in some areas will depend on the use of gas masks and oxygen tanks.

Scientists disagree as to the effect that man's present style of life will have on planetary temperatures. Some anticipate a new ice age that will greatly reduce the habitable portions of the planet. Others expect a warming trend that will melt the polar ice caps. If this occurs, the level of the oceans will rise enough to submerge many of the world's greatest cities.

As habitable space declines, and as both land and sea become less productive, population *cannot* continue to expand. Unless air and water pollution and the poisoning of our bodies through food greatly shorten life expectancy, hundreds of millions of people will have to starve before a new balance is achieved between population and food supply.

This is a depressing projection, and many will regard it as unduly pessimistic. Perhaps the efforts now being made here and there to check population growth through birth control will spread and become more successful. Perhaps agricultural technology will prevent massive crop failures and further deterioration of the soil. Perhaps international treaties can control fishing in order to assure an optimum supply for future generations. Perhaps people will stop using the oceans as the depository for wastes, find ways of avoiding oil spills or of cleaning them up, and cease poisoning the coastal areas with sewage and chemicals. Perhaps world wide efforts against air pollution will be successful, and the present planetary temperature will be maintained.

But projection of past trends does not give us much assurance along these lines. Short-term gains and local interests usually win out in competition with long-term advantages and the larger good. When immediate needs are a matter of survival itself, restraint for the sake of others is hard to foresee.

It is equally possible to argue that these projections are too optimistic. They ignore the fact that the crises in food and pollution and the exhaustion of resources come at a time when humankind is in possession of ultimate weapons. Since Hiroshima and Nagasaki we have known that the human race lives under the threat of total extinction. To our atomic arsenal we have added equally lethal chemical and bacteriological weapons. Thus far the balance of terror has worked. We survived the Cuban confrontation. We have exercised restraint in Vietnam. We may survive the still more serious crisis in the Middle East.

But as world population grows and resources decline, tensions will be heightened. The present tone of international relations will seem calm and relaxed in retrospect. In addition, more and more nations will gain possession of apocalyptic weapons. Can we expect a people facing a real threat of extinction to refrain from unleashing the ultimate weapon and allow its enemies to be victorious?

How do we react to this somber picture of our situation? I shall speak for myself in the belief that others resemble me. My first reaction is refusal of serious belief. The individual facts I may not be able to dispute, but I deny to myself that the situation is really that bad. The authorities, with all the power and knowledge at their disposal, will certainly take care of it. I shall put in my two cents' worth on this issue, as on others, to salve my conscience and to bolster my self-image as a concerned citizen, but beyond that I shall conduct business as usual, assuming that the future will be much like the past, putting out of my mind the apocalyptic threat under which we live.

However, there are times when the recognition of the planet's dying breaks through my defenses. Then my reaction tends to be one of despair. If all the present trends lead toward destruction, must I not realistically accept the early end of human life as inevitable? What use is it to attempt the impossible task of altering the course of history, especially when my influence is so slight?

It is important to recognize the great similarity of these two responses of complacency and despair. Their results are almost identical. They let *me* off the hook. I am left free to eat, drink, and be merry—or more realistically, to enjoy my family, my friends, and my work—for there is no real problem to whose solution I am called to contribute. Either others will solve it or it is insoluble. My attention can be directed toward the immediate and manageable issues of daily living.

Realistic hope represents a third alternative to complacency and despair. Those who hope can view the threat unflinchingly. They do not deny its seriousness either in their thoughts or in their feelings. Yet their hope is the refusal of despair. Those who hope seek openings, assume responsibility, endure failure after failure, and still seek new openings for fresh efforts.

In the depths of a depression Franklin Delano Roosevelt once said that the only thing we had to fear was fear itself. Today, facing the many trends that hurl us toward the abyss, we might say analogously, our only hope is hope itself. If we react in complacency or despair, there is no hope for human survival. If, instead, we hope, the future lies before us, full of uncertainties and risks, yet containing also hope.

But how can there be hope? To tell ourselves to hope in order that there be hope is, in the long run, futile. Hope rests on something other than its own usefulness. A partial answer is that hope is a matter of temperament or disposition, something to be dealt with, if at all, by psychologists. Perhaps such a temperament is closely connected with the basic trust one develops in the early months of one's life when one is fortunate in one's maternal care.

But there are other dimensions of hope, dimensions we can call existential, or religious, or even theological. In some measure hope is a function of what we believe, and in this global crisis, it is a function of what we believe *ultimately and comprehensively.*

The Old Testament found hope in the anticipated interventions of a transcendent God. The New Testament looked forward to the apocalyptic end of an unacceptable history. Few of us can live with these visions of reality, and their collapse in the last three centuries seems to have removed the grounds of hope for many people. In much of our youth culture, hope is focused on short-term goals, and it is easily shattered when these are not realized. The quest for kicks, or mystical meaning, or celebration of life in the present moment, are, in part, an expression of the loss of hope, a loss we older people have bequeathed to our children. Is there, nevertheless, for us also a basis of hope somehow equivalent to that of the Bible?

I cannot speak here for all, or for all religious people, or even for all Christians. But for myself the answer is "yes." The fact that when chemical conditions make it possible life appears, with growth and reproduction, means to me that there is that in reality that calls life forth and forward and strives against the forces of inertia and death. The fact that the human psyche is capable of being claimed by truth and touched by concern for fellow human beings means to me that there is that in reality that calls forth honesty and love and strives against the retreat into security, narrow interests, and merely habitual behavior. This power works slowly and quietly by persuasion without calling attention to itself. It does not present itself for observation by biologists or psychologists. Yet, it is presupposed in both the organisms they study and in their own faithful pursuit of truth. It is not to be found somewhere outside the organisms in which it is at work, but it is not to be identified with them either. We can conceive it best as Spirit.

It is the belief in this Spirit, the giver of life and love, that is the basis of hope. In spite of all the destructive forces we let loose against life on this planet, the Spirit of Life is at work in ever new and unforeseeable ways, countering and circumventing the obstacles we put in its path. In spite of my strong tendencies to complacency and despair, I experience the Spirit in myself as calling forth the realistic hope apart from which there is no hope, and I am confident that what I find in myself is occurring in others also.

Since what makes for life and love and hope is not simply the decision of one individual or another, but a Spirit that moves us all, I do not have to suppose that my own efforts are of great consequence in order to believe them to be worthwhile. I can recognize that they may even be futile or misdirected and still persist in them as long as no clearer light is given, for I see what I do as part of something much greater, something in which all persons participate to whatever extent they sensitively respond to the insights and opportunities that come their way. Belief in the Spirit is belief that I am not alone, that in working for life and love in hope, I am working *with* something much greater than myself, that there are possibilities for the future that cannot be simply projected out of the past, that even my mistakes and failures may be woven into a healing pattern of which I am not now aware.

Belief in the Spirit is no ground for complacency. There is no guarantee that people will respond to the Spirit's promptings in sufficient numbers and with sufficient sensitivity to begin the healing of the planet. But there is the possibility. The future *can* be different from the past. Therefore there is hope. Where there is life, there *is* hope.

Now we have returned full circle. We asked whether all this talk of changing attitudes, developing a new consciousness, and belief in God was worthwhile when the practical tasks at hand are so urgent. Is it not perhaps too late? If we have hope it may not be, but if we despair, then there is indeed no hope. When we asked how such hope can endure, we found ourselves grounding it in belief in Spirit. That Spirit, of course, is the God of whom we have been speaking. It is because of God that it may not be too late.

Afterword

This book was written in the summer of 1970. It expressed my first awakening to the environmental crisis. Rereading it now makes me realize how little, basically, my response has changed in the ensuing years.

Of course, if I were writing now, much would be different. What I wrote in 1970 was formed by the events of the sixties. Also there was a plethora of dire predictions among which it was not always easy to distinguish realistic projections from exaggerated alarmism. Some elements of the latter show up in the text.

The alarmism affects especially the timing. In a number of ways deterioration has not occurred as fast as I then feared. This is partly because of positive responses that have been made to various threats, but it is partly also that I underestimated the resiliency of nature. On the other hand, I was ignorant of whole dimensions of the danger, such as ozone depletion.

My language has changed since I wrote this book. About three years later I finally acknowledged that using only male language was truly oppressive of women, and I began the process of cleaning up my act. Reading this book, again I was appalled by how pervasive sexist language was. I have worked through the manuscript to remove most of this, although I have left the quotes and closely related material alone. Also, where the use of male language seems appropriate to what was said, I occasionally left it. This change constitutes the only significant way in which the text has been updated.

A few years after writing this book, I also gave up the term *subhuman* to refer to the nonhuman world. The reasons are, I think, obvious. Even if I continue to think that the human species is the most remarkable and intrinsically valuable among the creatures, other species should not be described as *sub*human. I have, therefore, substituted the more neutral term *nonhuman*.

My understanding of primal peoples has also changed. For this I am especially indebted to the influence of Paul Shepard. I have not been persuaded that primal existence constitutes the norm by which all others are to be judged, but I am convinced that civilized people have drastically undervalued the quality of primal life, and a number of my statements in this book continue that pejorative tradition. But that, too, stands unchanged in the text.

I have thought a great deal since writing this book about the changes that are needed if we are to avoid destruction. My reflections have drawn me especially into economics. From my present point of view, some of the proposals made here seem simplistic and naive. But there is little that I would directly reject.

The question that is the title of the book is still a burning one for me. Is it too late? The answer is that for many things it is already too late. That is, there were possibilities for a happy future in 1970 that no longer exist today. Perhaps this is clearest with respect to ozone depletion and its consequences. We do not yet know the full extent of those destructive effects of this depletion that are now strictly inevitable. But we do know that it is too late to save our children from seriously adverse consequences.

Assuming that although very serious, ozone depletion alone will not cause the whole life-support system of the planet to unravel, the question remains whether there is still time to salvage enough of that system from the abuse we continue to inflict upon it in other ways, so that our descendants can have a decent life. I do not know. Certainly, if we continue to aim at increasing production as our major global goal, as all national governments and both political parties in this country still do, only disaster can await us. Perhaps the forces at work in this respect cannot be stopped before they destroy us.

Perhaps it is too late. But whereas there is no way of stopping the chemicals that damage the ozone layer from continuing their upward journey, there are ways of redirecting our economic energies away from growth toward meeting real needs. The problem here is that there is not the understanding or the will.

Yet much that has happened since 1970 *is* encouraging. Although change has come far more slowly than I hoped when I wrote this book, it has come. The condition of the environment is universally recognized as *an* important issue. Most Americans assert that they are willing to make *some* economic adjustments for the sake of preserving or restoring a healthy environment. The world's most populous nation has taken drastic steps to curb its population growth. The second most populous nation has made serious, although thus far unsuccessful, efforts to do so.

The governments of the world did show that they are capable of taking serious action on environmental issues when they acted on ozone-destroying chemicals. The action was not as drastic as I would wish, and it was much too late to save the world from horrendous consequences of our carelessness. Nevertheless, when the evidence of the damage was overwhelming, the nations acted with some dispatch and decisiveness. This shows that dispatch and decisiveness *may* characterize action on other, equally important, issues in the future.

Preparing environmental impact reports on proposed activities has become widespread practice. Belatedly this requirement was introduced into the World Bank. That there is much evasion, deception, and corruption with respect to these, and that they are widely ignored, cannot be denied. But their existence is another important sign of a shift in public thinking, and they have made an important difference.

The word *sustainable,* introduced into public discourse by the World Council of Churches at Nairobi in 1975, is now central to the rhetoric of economic development. Most of those who use it continue to recommend policies that are in fact wholly unsustainable. But their acceptance, in principle, of the idea provides a basis for critical reflection and for discussion of these policies. This could begin to affect policies before long.

A United States senator who has become vice-president has written a book that shows a fundamentally accurate understanding of the environmental crisis and its importance. This means that discussions that have thus far occurred only at the fringes of politics may move toward center.

It would be possible to list other encouraging signs of change. It would also be possible to point to much that is profoundly disappointing and discouraging. The fate of the Earth remains unsure.

This book was written for lay use in the church. The series of which it was part was specifically for Roman Catholics, although I am myself a Protestant. That I was asked to write for that audience, and that the book was published despite the position it takes on population issues, shows something of the ecumenical climate of those years following on Vatican II.

In this respect and others, the years since then have not been happy ones for the churches. On the other hand, there has been some progress with respect to the sort of issues dealt with in this book. The World Council of Churches has given positive leadership. The emphasis in its formulations has shifted from being purely anthropocentric to including the whole of creation in the sphere of Christian concern. Many denominational statements have reflected this change, and a few are excellent. At the theological level to which this book was most directly addressed, changes in official formulations among the oldline churches are encouraging.

Partly because of the decline in the general health of these churches, however, the effect of these changes among church people and within local churches is still very modest. Most church people are still shaped in their environmental views more by the newspaper and television than by their faith and worship. Theological education for lay people lags very seriously indeed.

I am deeply grateful to Eugene Hargrove and *Environmental Ethics Books* for making this little book available again. I was assured that earlier it was useful in church study groups. Perhaps it can be useful in that context again. I believe that most of it is relevant for the general public as well.

Notes

Chapter 1: "What's the Problem?"
[1] Richard M. Nixon, "State of the Union Message," 1970.
Chapter 2: "Is Ecology the Issue?"
[1] George Perkins Marsh, *Man and Nature,* ed. David Lowenthal (Cambridge, Mass.: Belknap Press of Harvard University Press, 1965), pp. 42–43.
[2] *Esquire,* September 1967, pp. 116–18.
[3] *Brookhaven Biology Symposium, 1969.*
[4] *Los Angeles Times.*
Chapter 3: "Let the Engineers Handle It!"
[1] "Fighting to Save the Earth from Man," *Time,* 2 February 1970.
Chapter 4: "The Christian Responsibility"
[1] Lynn White, Jr., "The Historical Roots of Our Ecological Crisis," *Science,* 10 March 1967, pp. 1203–07.
[2] Ibid.
[3] Aldo Leopold, *A Sand County Almanac* (New York: Ballantine Books, 1970), p. 245.
Chapter 5: "Non-Western Views of Nature"
[1] Theodore Roszak, *The Making of a Counter Culture* (Garden City, N.Y.: Doubleday & Co., 1969), p. 258.
[2] Ibid., p. 245.
[3] Stewart Udall, *The Quiet Crisis* (New York: Holt, Rinehart & Winston, 1964), p. 4.
[4] Ernest Cassirer, *An Essay on Man* (Garden City, N.Y.: Doubleday & Co., Anchor Book, 1953), p. 109.
[5] Erich Neumann, *The Origins and History of Consciousness,* 2 vols. (New York: Harper & Brothers Torchbook, 1954), p. 40.
[6] George Foot Moore, *History of Religions,* vol. 1 (New York: Charles Scribner's Sons, 1946), p. 55.
[7] "Tao Teh King, #34," in S. E. Frost, ed., *The Sacred Writings of the World's Great Religions* (New York: The New Home Library, 1943). Available as *Tao Te Ching,* trans. D. C. Lau (Baltimore, Md.: Penguin Books, 1963).
[8] Marsh, *Man and Nature,* pp. 35–36.
Chapter 6: "A New Christianity"
[1] Albert Schweitzer, *Out of My Life and Thought,* ed. C. T. Campion (New York: New American Library, Mentor Books, 1953), p. 126.
[2] Leopold, *A Sand County Almanac,* p. 254.
Chapter 9: "Nature as Historic"
[1] Quoted in Udall, "Introduction," *The Quiet Crisis,* pp. xi–xii.
[2] "A Christological View of Nature," *Religious Education* 67 (January–February 1971), p. 37.
Chapter 10: "Humanity as Part of Nature"
[1] Albrecht B. Ritschl, *The Christian Doctrine of Justification and Reconciliation,* 2d ed., trans. H. R. Mackintosh and A. B. Macaulay (Edinburgh: T. & T. Clark, 1902), p. 199.
Chapter 11: "Is the Nonhuman World Real?"
[1] George Perkins Marsh, quoted in Udall, *The Quiet Crisis,* p. 71.
Chapter 13: "Whitehead: An Ecological Philosophy"
[1] Alfred North Whitehead, *Science and the Modern World* (New York: New American Library, Mentor Books, 1948), p. 175.
[2] Ibid., p. 180.
Chapter 14: "The Commitment We Need"
[1] In *Poetical Works of Matthew Arnold* (New York: Macmillan, 1910), p. 5.

Bibliography of Christian
Theology and Ecology

This bibliography of English-language material is based largely on selections from half a dozen other bibliographies supplemented by some independent research. It is fairly thorough through 1991, progressively less so for the years thereafter. I have not listed individual essays which are contained in books included in the bibliography, in special issues of journals listed at the end, or in the magazines, also listed at the end, which have large numbers of relevant pieces. By far the most detailed bibliography in this field is that by Joseph Sheldon, listed below.

Abrecht, Paul. "Impact of Science and Technology on Society: New Directions in Ecumenical Social Ethics." *Zygon*, September 1977, pp. 185–98.

———, ed. *Faith, Science, and the Future.* Geneva: World Council of Churches, 1978.

Adams, Carol J., ed. *Ecofeminism and the Sacred.* New York: Continuum, 1993.

Ahlers, Julia. "Thinking Like a Mountain: toward a Sensible Land Ethic." *Christian Century,* 25 April 1990, pp. 433–34.

Ajakaiye, D. Enilo and Jonathan King. "First World, Third World: Uses and Abuses of Science." *Christianity and Crisis,* 27 October 1980, pp. 298–303.

Allerton, John. "About a Theology of Conservation." *Faith and Freedom,* Autumn 1985, pp. 114–26.

Alpers, K. P. "Toward an Environmental Ethic." *Dialog,* Winter 1976, pp. 49–55.

American Lutheran Church. *The Land: Statements and Actions of the American Lutheran Church (1978–1982) Dealing with the Land and Those Who Tend It.* Minneapolis: Augsburg, 1982.

Anderson, Bernhard W. "Exodus Typology in Second Isaiah." *Israel's Prophetic Heritage,* ed. Bernhard W. Anderson and Walter Harrelson, New York: Harper, 1962, pp. 177–95.

———. "Human Dominion Over Nature." *Biblical Studies in Contemporary Thought,* ed. Miriam Ward. Somerville, Mass.: Greeno, Hadden and Co., 1975, pp. 27–45.

———. *Creation in the Old Testament.* Philadelphia: Fortress Press, 1984.

Ashley, Benedict. "Dominion or Stewardship? Theological Reflections." *Birth, Suffering and Death,* ed. Kevin W. Wildes, et al. Boston: Kluwer Academic Publications, 1992, pp. 85–106.

Asselin, D. T. "The Notion of Dominion in Genesis 1–3." *Catholic Biblical Quarterly,* July 1954, pp. 277–94.

Attfield, Robin. "Christian Attitudes to Nature." *Journal of the History of Ideas,* July–September 1983, pp. 369–86.

Austin, Richard Cartwright. "Three Axioms for Land Use." *Christian Century,* 12 October 1977, pp. 910–11, 915.

———. "Toward Environmental Theology." *Drew Gateway,* Winter 1977, pp. 1–14.

———. *Baptized into Wilderness.* Atlanta: John Knox Press, 1987.

———. *Hope for the Land: Nature in the Bible.* Atlanta: John Knox Press, 1988.

———. *Beauty of the Lord: Awakening the Senses.* Atlanta: John Knox Press, 1988.

Baer, Richard A, Jr. "Land Misuse: A Theological Concern." *Christian Century,* 12 October 1966, pages 1239–41.

———. "Conservation: An Area for the Church's Concern." *Christian Century,* 8 January 1969, pp. 40–43.

———. "Ecology, Religion and the American Dream." *American Ecclesiastical Review,* September 1971, pp. 43–59.

Bailey, L. H. *The Holy Earth.* New York: Macmillan, 1923.

Balasuriya, Tissa. *Planetary Theology.* London: SCM Press, 1984.

Ballard, Paul H. "Conservation in a Christian Context." *Baptist Quarterly,* January 1985, pp. 23–38.

Barbour, Ian. "An Ecological Ethic." *Christian Century,* 7 October 1970, pp. 1180–84.

————, ed. *Earth Might Be Fair: Reflections on Ethics, Religion and Ecology.* Englewood Cliffs, N.J.: Prentice Hall, 1972.

————, ed. *Western Man and Environmental Ethics: Attitudes toward Nature and Technology.* Reading, Mass.: Addison-Wesley Publishing Co., 1973.

————. *Technology, Environment and Human Values.* New York: Praeger, 1980.

————. "Response to Panel on 'The Church and the Environmental Crisis.'" *CTNS Bulletin,* Autumn 1990, pp. 26–28.

————. *Religion in an Age of Science: The Gifford Lectures 1989-1991,* vol. 1. San Francisco: Harper and Row, 1990.

————. *Ethics in an Age of Technology: The Gifford Lectures*, vol. 2. San Francisco: Harper and Row, 1993.

Barclay, Oliver R. "Animal Rights: a Critique." *Science and Christian Belief*, April 1992, pp. 49–61.

Barnes, Michael, ed. *An Ecology of the Spirit: Religious Reflection and Environmental Consciousness.* Lanham, Md.: University Press of America, 1994.

Barnette, Henlee H. *The Church and the Ecological Crisis.* Grand Rapids, Mich.: Wm. B. Eerdmans, 1972.

Barr, James. "The Images of God in the Book of Genesis." *Bulletin of the John Rylands University Library,* Autumn 1968–69, pp. 11–28.

————. "Man and Nature: the Ecological Controversy and the Old Testament." *Bulletin of the John Rylands University Library,* Autumn 1972, pp. 9–32.

Bauckham, Richard. "First Step to a Theology of Nature." *Evangelical Quarterly,* July 1986, pp. 229–44.

Becker, William H. "Ecological Sin." *Theology Today,* July 1992, pp. 152–64.

Beisner, E. Calvin. *Prospects for Growth: a Biblical View of Population, Resources and the Future.* Westchester, Ill.: Crossway Books, 1990.

Benjamin, W. W. "A Challenge to the Eco-Doomsters." *Christian Century*, 21 March 1979, pp. 252–72.

Bennett, John B. "Nature—God's Body: A Whiteheadian Perspective." *Philosophy Today,* Fall 1974, pp. 248–54.

————. "A Context for the Land Ethic." *Philosophy Today,* Summer 1976, pp. 124–33.

————. "On Responding to Lynn White: Ecology and Christianity." *Ohio Journal of Religious Studies,* April 1977, pp. 71–77.

Berry, Robert J. *Ecology and Ethics.* Downers Grove, Ill.: Inter-Varsity Press, 1972.

————. "Christianity and the Environment: Escapist Mysticism or Responsible Stewardship." *Science and Christian Belief,* April 1991, pp. 3–18.

Berry, Thomas. "Wonderworld as Wasteworld: The Earth in Deficit." *CrossCurrents,* Winter 1985/86, pp. 408–22.

————. *The Dream of the Earth.* San Francisco: Sierra Club Books, 1988.

————, Thomas Clar, Stephen Dunn, and Anne Lonergan, eds. *Befriending the Earth: A Theology of Reconciliation between Humans and the Earth.* Mystic, CT: Twenty-Third Publications, 1991.

Berry, Wendell. "The Gift of Good Land." *The Gift of Good Land: Further Essays Cultural and Agricultural.* San Francisco: North Point Press, 1981, pp. 267–81.

————. "Two Economies." *Review and Expositor,* Spring 1984, pp. 209–23.

————. "Christianity and the Survival of Creation." *CrossCurrents,* Summer 1993, pp. 149–63.

Best, Bruce. "The A to Z of Everything." *One World,* April 1981, pp. 17–19.

Bhagat, Shantilal. *Creation in Crisis: Responding to God's Covenant.* Elgin, Ill.: Brethren Press, 1990.

Biggs, John. "Toward a Theology for the Environment." *Baptist Quarterly,* January 1991, pp. 33–42.

Birch, Bruce C. "Energy Ethics Reaches the Church's Agenda." *Christian Century,* November 1978, pp. 1034–38.

————, and Larry Rasmussen. *The Predicament of the Prosperous.* Philadelphia: Westminster Press, 1978.

Birch, Charles. *Nature and God.* Philadelphia: Westminster Press, 1965.

————. "Three Facts, Eight Fallacies and Three Axioms about Population and Environment." *Ecumenical Review,* January 1973, pp. 29–40.

————. "Creation, Technology and Human Survival: Called to Replenish the Earth." *Ecumenical Review,* January 1976, pp. 66–79.

————. "Nature, God and Humanity in Ecological Perspective." *Christianity and Crisis,* 29 October 1979, pp. 259–66.

————, and John B. Cobb, Jr. *The Liberation of Life: From the Cell to the Community.* Cambridge, England: Cambridge University Press, 1981; Denton, Tex.: Environmental Ethics Books, 1990.

————. "How Brave a New World?" *Ecumenical Review,* January 1985, pp. 152–60.

————. "The Scientific-Environmental Crisis: Where Do the Churches Stand?" *Ecumenical Review,* April 1988, pp. 185–93.

————, William Eakin, and Jay B. McDaniel, eds. *Liberating Life: Contemporary Approaches to Ecological Theology.* Maryknoll, N.Y.: Orbis Books, 1990.

————. *On Purpose.* Kensington, Australia: New South Wales University Press, 1990. Also published as *A Purpose for Everything.* Mystic, Conn.: Twenty-Third Publications, 1990.

————. *Regaining Compassion for Humanity and Nature.* Kensington, Australia: New South Wales University Press, 1993 (also published by Chalice Press).

Birkenfeld, D. L. "Land: a Place Where Justice, Peace and Creation Meet." *International Review of Mission,* April 1989, pp. 155–61.

Bishop, Steve and Christopher Droop. *The Earth is the Lord's.* Bristol, Great Britian: Regius Press, 1990.

Black, John. *The Dominion of Man: The Search for Ecological Responsibility.* Edinburgh: University of Edinburgh Press, 1970.

Blackburn, Joyce. *The Earth is the Lord's?* Waco, Tex.: Word Books, 1972.

Blair, Ian. "Energy and Environment: The Ecological Debate." *The Year 2000,* ed. John R. W. Stott. Downers Grove, Ill.: InterVarsity Press, 1983, pp. 103–25.

Blancy, Alain. "Economic Growth and the Quality of Life." *Ecumenical Review*, July 1976, pp. 296–307.

Blewett, J. "The Greening of Catholic Social Thought." *Pro Mundi Vita Studies,* February 1990, pp. 27-35.

Blidstein, G. J. "Man and Nature in the Sabbatical Year," *Tradition,* vol. 9, no. 4, 1966, pp. 48–55.

Bluck, John. "The Great Debate." *One World,* September 1979, pp. 11–16.

Bockmuhl, K. *Conservation and Lifestyle,* trans. B. N. Kaye. Bramcote, Notts., Great Britian.: Grove Books, 1977.

Bonifazi, Conrad. *A Theology of Things: A Study of Man in His Physical Environment.* Philadelphia: Lippincott, 1967.

————. *The Soul of the World: An Account of the Inwardness of Things.* Lanham, Md.: University Press of America, 1978.

Booty, John. "Tradition, Traditions and the Present Global Crisis." *No Easy Path,* ed. Carter Heywood and Sue Phillips. Lanham, Md.: University Press of America, 1992, pp. 73–90.

Bordo, Jonathan. "Ecological Peril, Modern Technology, and the Postmodern Sublime." *Shadow of Spirit,* ed. Philippa Berry and Andrew Warwick. London: Routledge, 1991, pp. 132–46.

Bouma-Prediger, Steve. "Why Should I Care for Creation? A Half Dozen or So Arguments." *Perspectives: A Journal of Reformed Thought,* May 1993, pp. 8–11.

Bowman, Douglas C. *Beyond the Modern Mind: The Spiritual and Ethical Challenge of the*

Environmental Crisis. New York: Pilgrim Press, 1990.

Braaten, Carl E. "Toward an Ecological Theology." Chap. 8 in *Christ and Counter-Christ: Apocalyptic Themes in Theology and Culture.* Philadelphia: Fortress Press, 1972.

———. "Caring for the Future: Where Ethics and Ecology Meet." Chap. 12 in *Eschatology and Ethics.* Minneapolis: Augsburg, 1974.

Bradley, Ian. *God is Green: Christianity and the Environment.* London: Dalton, Longman and Todd, 1990.

Bratton, Susan Power. "The Ecotheology of James Watt." *Environmental Ethics,* Fall 1983, pp. 225–36.

———. "Christian Ecotheology and the Old Testament." *Environmental Ethics,* Fall 1984, pp. 195–209.

———. "The Original Desert Solitaire: Early Christian Monasticism and Wilderness." *Environmental Ethics,* Spring 1988, pp. 31–55.

———. "Teaching Environmental Ethics from a Theological Perspective." *Religious Education,* Winter 1990, pp. 25–33.

———. *Six Billion and More: Human Population Regulation and Christian Ethics.* Louisville: Westminster/John Knox Press, 1992.

———. "Loving Nature: Eros or Agape." *Environmental Ethics,* Spring 1992, pp. 3–25.

———. *Christianity, Wilderness, and Wildlife: the Original Desert Solitaire.* Scranton, Pa.: Scranton University Press, 1993.

———. "Ecofeminism and the Problem of Divine Immanence/Transcendence in Christian Environmental Ethics." *Science and Christian Belief,* April 1994, pp. 21–46.

Breuilly, Elizabeth and Martin Palmer, eds. *Christianity and Ecology.* London: World Wildlife Fund and Cassell, 1992.

Brisbin, I. L. "The Principles of Ecology as a Frame of Reference for Ethical Challenges: Towards the Development of an Ecological Theology." *Georgia Journal of Science,* vol. 37, 1979, pp. 21–34.

Brown, Noel J. and Pierre Quiblier, eds. *Ethics and Agenda 21: Moral Implications of Global Consensus.* New York: United Nations Environment Program, 1994.

Bruce, F. F. "The Bible and the Environment." *The Living and Active Word of God: Studies in Honor of Samuel J. Schultz,* ed. Morris Inch and Ronald Youngblood. Winona Lake, Ind.: Eisenbrauns, 1983.

Brueggemann, Walter. "King in the Kingdom of Things." *Christian Century,* 10 September 1969, pp. 1165–66.

———. *The Land: Place as Gift, Promise and Challenge in Biblical Faith.* Philadelphia: Fortress Press, 1977.

———. "On Land Losing and Land Receiving." *Dialog,* Spring 1980, pp. 166–73.

———. *Living toward a Vision: Biblical Reflections on Shalom.* New York: United Church Press, 1982.

———. *Genesis: A Bible Commentary for Teaching and Preaching.* Atlanta: John Knox Press, 1982.

———. *Interpretation: Genesis.* Atlanta: John Knox Press, 1983.

———. "Theses on Land in the Bible." *The Church and Appalachian Land Issues,* ed. Erets. Amesville, Ohio: Coalition for Appalachian Ministry, 1984.

———. "The Earth is the Lord's." *Sojourners,* October 1986, pp. 28–32.

———. "The Land and Our Urban Appetites." *Perspectives: A Journal of Reformed Thought,* February 1989, pp. 9–13.

———. *Using God's Resources Wisely: Isaiah and Urban Possibility,* Louisville: Westminster/ John Knox, 1993.

Bruteau, Beatrice. "Eucharistic Ecology and Ecological Spirituality." *CrossCurrents,* Winter 1990–1991, pp. 449–514.

Bugbee, Henry. "Wilderness in America." *Journal of the American Academy of Religion,* December 1974, pp. 614–20.

Byron, William J., S.J. *Toward Stewardship: An Interim Ethic of Poverty, Power and Pollution.* New York: Paulist Press, 1975.

Callicott, J. Baird. "Genesis and John Muir." *ReVision,* Winter 1990, pp. 31–46.

Campbell, J. B. "Our Common Future." *Church and Society,* September-October 1990, pp. 31–40.

Carmody, John. *Ecology and Religion: Toward a New Christian Theology of Nature.* New York/Ramsey, N.J.: Paulist Press, 1983.

Carothers, J. Edward, Margaret Mead, Daniel D. McCracken, and Roger L. Shinn, eds. *To Love or to Perish: the Technological Crisis and the Churches.* New York: Friendship Press, 1972.

———. *Caring for the World.* New York: Friendship Press, 1978.

Carpenter, Edward. *Animals and Ethics.* London: Watkins, 1980.

Carpenter, James A. *Nature and Grace.* New York: Crossroads, 1988.

Carroll, Dennis. *Towards a Story of the Earth: Essays in the Theology of Creation.* Dublin: Dominican Publications, 1987.

———. "On Not Jumping on the Green Bandwagon." *Ethics and the Christian,* ed. Sean Freyne. Dublin: Columba Press, 1991, pp. 127–37.

Catholic Bishops (Philippines). "What is Happening to Our Beautiful Land? *Sedos Bulletin,* 15 April 1988, pp. 112–15.

Cauthen, Kenneth. "The Case for Christian Biopolitics." *Christian Century,* 19 November 1969, pp. 1481–83.

———. *Christian Biopolitics: A Credo and Strategy for the Future.* Nashville: Abingdon Press, 1971.

———. "Ecojustice: A Future-Oriented Strategy of Ministry and Mission." *Foundations,* April–June 1973, pp. 156–70.

———. *The Ethics of Enjoyment.* Atlanta: John Knox Press, 1975.

———. *Process Ethics: A Constructive System.* New York: Edwin Mellen Press, 1984.

———. "Imagining the Future: New Visions and New Responsibilities." *Zygon,* September 1985, pp. 321–39.

Cesaretti, C. A. and Stephen Commins, eds. *Let the Earth Bless the Lord: A Christian Perspective on Land Use.* New York: Seabury Press, 1981.

Chappell, David, ed. "Ecological Crisis." *Buddhist Christian Studies,* 1992, pp. 161–78.

Christiansen, Andrew. "Notes on Moral Theology, 1989; Ecology, Justice, and Development." *Theological Studies,* March 1990, pp. 64–81.

Church of England (Board of Social Responsibility). *Man in His Living Environment: An Ethical Assessment.* London: Church House Publishing, 1970.

——— (Report of the General Synod). *Our Responsibility for the Living Environment.* London: Church House Publishing, 1986.

Church of Scotland (Society, Religion and Technology Project). *While Earth Endures.* SRT Project/Quorum Press, 1986.

Clampit, M. K. "The Ecological Covenant and Nature as a Sacred Symbol." *Religious Education,* May–June 1972, pp. 194–98.

Clark, J. Michael. *Beyond Our Ghettoes: Gay Theology in Ecological Perspective.* Cleveland: Pilgrim Press, 1994.

Clark, Susan J. *Celebrating Earth Holy Days: A Resource Guide for Faith Communities.* New York: Crossroad, 1992.

Clifford, Richard J. "The Hebrew Scriptures and the Theology of Creation." *Theological Studies,* September 1985, pp. 507–23.

Clinebell, Howard J. "Enhancing Your Well-Being by Helping Heal a Wounded Planet." Chap. 8 in *Well-Being: A Personal Plan for Exploring and Enriching the Seven Dimensions of Life: Mind, Body, Spirit, Love, Work, Play, Earth.* San Francisco: Harper San Francisco, 1992.

Cobb, Clifford W. "Food and the Christian Faith." *Religion in Life,* Spring 1980, pp. 65–71.

Cobb, John B. Jr. *Is It Too Late? A Theology of Ecology.* Beverley Hills, Calif.: Bruce, 1972.

———. "Ecology, Ethics, and Theology." *Toward a Steady-State Economy,* ed. Herman E. Daly.

San Francisco: W. H. Freeman. 1973, pp. 307–20. (Also included in the revised and expanded version: *Economics, Ecology, Ethics: Essays toward a Steady-State Economy,* 1980.)

———. "The Christian, the Future, and Paolo Soleri." *Christian Century,* 30 October 1974, pp. 1008–11.

———, and David R. Griffin. "The Global Crisis and a Theology of Survival." Chap. 9 in *Process Theology: An Introductory Exposition.* Philadelphia: Westminster Press 1976.

———. "Beyond Anthropocentrism in Ethics and Religion." *On the Fifth Day,* ed. Richard Knowles Morris and Michael W. Fox. Washington: Acropolis Books, 1978, pp. 137–53.

———. "Process Theology and Environmental Issues." *Journal of Religion,* October 1980, pp. 440–58.

———. "Sociological Theology or Ecological Theology." Chap. 6 of *Process Theology as Political Theology.* Philadelphia: The Westminster Press, 1982.

———. "A Christian View of Biodiversity." *Biodiversity,* ed. E. O. Wilson. Washington: National Academy Press, 1988, pp. 481–85.

———. "The Earth and Humanity: A Christian View." *Three Faiths—One God,* ed. John Hick and Edmund S. Meltzer. London: Macmillan, 1989, pp. 113–28.

———. *Can Christ Become Good News Again?* St. Louis: Chalice Press, 1991.

———. "The Right to Kill." Chap. 1 in *Matters of Life and Death.* Louisville: Westminster/John Knox, 1991.

———. *Sustainability: Economics, Ecology, and Justice.* Maryknoll, N.Y.: Orbis Press, 1992.

———. "Biblical Responsibility for the Ecological Crisis." *Second Opinion,* October 1992, pp. 11–22.

———. "Theology and Ecology." *Colloquium,* May 1993, pp. 2–9.

———. *Sustaining the Common Good: A Christian Perspective on the Global Economy.* Cleveland: Pilgrim Press, 1994.

Cohen, Jeremy. "The Bible, Man and Nature in the History of Western Thought: A Call for Reassessment." *Journal of Religion,* April 1985, pp. 155–72.

———. *"Be Fertile and Increase, Fill the Earth and Master It": The Ancient and Medieval Career of a Biblical Text.* Ithaca, N.Y.: Cornell University Press, 1989.

Compton, Edward. "A Plea for a Theology of Nature." *Modern Churchman,* Winter 1978/79, pp. 3–11.

Cooper, Tim and D. Kemball-Cook, eds. *God's Green World.* Malvern, Worc., Great Britian: Christian Ecology Group, 1983.

———. *Green Christianity: Caring for the Whole Creation.* London: Hodder and Stoughton, 1990.

Crumbey, C. *The Hidden Dangers of the Rainbow: The New Age Movement and Our Coming Age of Barbarism.* Shreveport, La.: Huntington House, 1983.

Cummings, Charles. "Exploring Eco-Spirituality." *Spirituality Today,* vol. 41, 1989, pp. 30–41.

———. *Eco-Spirituality: Toward a Reverent Life.* Mahwah, N.J.: Paulist Press, 1991.

Daetz, Douglas. "Heading Off Eco-Catastrophe: A Job for New Adam." *Lutheran Quarterly,* August 1970, pp. 271–78.

———. "No More Business as Usual." *Dialog,* Summer 1970, pp. 171–75.

Dalton, Mary A. "Befriending an Estranged Home." *Religious Education,* Winter 1990, pp. 15–24.

Daly, Herman E. *Steady State Economics.* San Francisco: W. H. Freeman, 1977.

———, and John B. Cobb, Jr. *For the Common Good: Redirecting the Economy toward Community, the Environment, and a Sustainable Future.* Boston: Beacon Press, 1989. (Revised 1994.)

Damaskinos, Met. of Switzerland. "Man and His Environment: The Ecological Problem: Its Positive and Negative Aspects." *Journal of the Moscow Patriarchate,* Summer 1990, pp. 412–23.

Dannel, M. L. "Towards a Sacramental Theology of the Environment in African Independent Churches." *Theologia Evangelica,* March 1991, pp. 2–26.

Davidson, Doug. "Learning from the Land." *Other Side,* January-February 1992, pp. 8–11.

De la Cruz, A. "Scriptural Basis of Ecology: A Mandate for Environmental Stewardship." *Taiwan Journal of Theology,* vol. 10, 1988, pp. 211–23.

Denig, N. W. "'On Values' Revisited: A Judeo-Christian Theology of Man and Nature." *Landscape Journal,* vol. 4, no. 2, 1985, pp. 96–105.

Derr, Thomas Sieger. "Man Against Nature." *Cross Currents,* Summer 1970, pp. 263–75.

———. *Ecology and Human Need.* Philadelphia: Westminster Press, 1975. (Originally published as *Ecology and Human Liberation: A Theological Critique of the Use and Abuse of Our Birthright.* New York: WSCF Books, 1973.)

———. "Religion's Responsibility for the Ecological Crisis: An Argument Run Amok." *Worldview,* January 1975, pp. 39–45.

———. "Science and Technology." *Ecumenical Review,* April 1976, pp. 131–40.

Derrick, Christopher. *The Delicate Creation: Towards a Theology of the Environment.* Old Greenwich, Conn.: Devin-Adair, 1972.

Devadas, David. "Work, Technology and the Environment." *One World,* April 1986, pp. 11–15.

Dew, W. H. "Religious Approach to Nature." *Church Quarterly Review,* vol. 150, 1950, pp. 81–89.

DeWitt, C. B. *A Sustainable Earth: Religion and Ecology in the Western Hemisphere.* Mancelona, Minn.: AuSable Institute of Environmental Studies, 1987.

———. "Seven Degradations of Creation." *Perspectives: A Journal of Reformed Thought,* February 1989, pp. 4–8.

———, ed. *The Environment and the Christian: What Does the New Testament Say About the Environment?* Grand Rapids, Mich.: Baker Book House, 1991.

———. "Christian Colleges at an Ecological Turning Point." *Faculty Dialogue,* Winter 1992, pp. 43–58.

——— and Ghillean T. Prance, eds. *Missionary Earthkeeping.* Atlanta: Mercer University Press, 1993.

DeWolf, L. Harold. "Our Natural Environment." Chap. 11 in *Responsible Freedom: Guidelines to Christian Action.* New York: Harper and Row, 1971.

———. "Theology and Ecology." *American Ecclesiastical Review,* March 1971, pp. 154–70.

Ditmanson, H. H. "The Call for a Theology of Creation." *Dialog,* Summer 1964, pp. 264–73.

Doan, Gilbert E. Jr. "Toward a Life-Style Environmentally Informed." *Lutheran Quarterly,* November 1971, pp. 305–16.

Doble, Patrick J. "Stewards of the Earth's Resources: A Christian Response to Ecology." *Christian Century,* October 12, 1977, pp. 906–09.

Dombrowski, Daniel A. *Hartshorne and the Metaphysics of Animal Rights.* Albany: State University of New York Press, 1988.

Donaldson, James. "America the Beautiful: Interdependence with Nature." *Foundations,* July–September 1976, pp. 238–56.

Douglas, David. "Wild Country and Wildlife: A Spiritual Preserve." *Christian Century,* 4–11 January 1984, pp. 11–13.

Douglass, Gordon K., ed. *Agricultural Sustainability in a Changing World Order.* Boulder: Westview Press, 1984.

———, and Jane Douglass. "Creation, Reformed Faith, and Sustainable Food Systems." *Reformed Faith and Economics,* ed. Robert L. Stivers. Lanham, Md.: University Press of America, 1989, pp. 117–44.

Dowd, Michael. *The Meaning of Life in the 1990's: An Ecological Christian Perspective.* Granville, Mass.: Living Earth Christian Fellowship, 1990.

———. *Earthspirit: A Handbook for Nurturing Ecological Christianity.* Mystic, Conn.: Twenty-Third Publications, 1991.

Dubos, Rene. *A God Within.* New York: Charles Scribner's, 1972.

———. *The Wooing of Earth.* New York: Charles Scribner's, 1980.

Duchrow, Ulrich. *Global Economy: A Confessional Issue for the Church?* Geneva: WCC

Publications, 1987.

——, and Gerhard Liedke. *Shalom: Biblical Perspectives on Creation, Justice, and Peace.* Geneva: WCC Publications, 1987.

Dumas, Andre. "The Ecological Crisis and the Doctrine of Creation." *Ecumenical Review,* January 1975, pp. 25–35.

——. "A Society Which Creates Justice: Three Themes but One Development." *Ecumenical Review,* July 1978, pp. 211–19.

——. "When Science Looks to Faith." *Ecumenical Review,* October 1979, pp. 388–93.

Duncan, Roger. "Adam and the Ark." *Encounter,* Spring 1976, pp. 189–97.

Dunlap-Berg. *The Environment.* Nashville: Abingdon Press, 1994.

Dunn, Stephen. "Ecology, Ethics, and the Religious Educator." *Religious Education,* Winter 1990, pp. 34–41.

——, and Anne Lonergan, eds. *Befriending the Earth: A Theology of Reconciliation Between Humans and the Earth.* Mystic, Conn.: Twenty-Third Publications, 1991.

Dwyer, Judith A. "Questions of Special Urgency: Ethical Dilemmas in the Third Millenium." *Theology toward the Third Millenium,* ed. David G. Schulteneuer. Lewiston, NY: Edwin Mellen Press, 1991, pp. 103–23.

Dyrness, William A. "Are We Our Planet's Keeper?" *Christianity Today,* 18 April 1991, pp. 40–42.

——. "Environmental Ethics and the Covenant of Hosea 2." *Studies in Old Testament Theology,* ed. Robert L. Hubbard, Jr. et al. Dallas: Word Publications, 1992, pp. 263–78.

Edinburgh, The Duke of, and Michael Mann. *Survival or Extinction: A Christian Attitude to the Environment.* Windsor Castle, England: St. George's House, 1989.

Edwards, Denis. "The Integrity of Creation: Catholic Social Teachings for an Ecological Age." *Pacifica,* June 1992, pp. 182–203.

——. *Made from Stardust: Exploring the Place of Human Beings within Creation.* San Francisco: Harper San Francisco, 1992.

——. "An Ecological Theology of the Trinity." *CTNS Bulletin,* Summer 1993, pp. 10–16.

——. *Jesus, the Wisdom of God: An Ecological Theology.* Maryknoll, N.Y.: Orbis Press, in press.

ELCA Environmental Task Force. "A Theological Basis for Earth Care." *Lutheran Forum,* May 1993, pp. 24–26.

Elder, Frederick. "Two Modern Doctrines of Nature." *The Religious Situation: 1969,* ed. Donald R. Cutler. Boston: Beacon Press, 1969.

——. *Crisis in Eden.* New York: Abingdon Press, 1970.

Elsdon, Ron. *Bent World: A Christian Response to the Environmental Crisis.* Downers Grove, Ill.: InterVarsity Press, 1981.

——. "A Still-bent World: Some Reflections on Current Environmental Problems." *Science and Christian Belief,* vol. 1, no. 2, 1989, pp. 99–121.

Elwood, D. J. "Primitivism or Technocracy: Must We Choose?" *Christian Century,* December 1, 1971, pp. 1413–18.

Engel, J. Ronald. "Teaching the Eco-justice Ethic: The Parable of the Billerica Dam." *Christian Century,* 13 May 1987, pp. 466–69.

——. "Ecology and Social Justice: The Search for a Public Environmental Ethic." *Issues of Justice: Social Sources and Religious Meaning,* ed. Warren R. Copeland and Roger D. Hatch. Macon, Ga.: Mercer University Press, 1988.

——, and Joan Gibb Engel, eds. *Ethics of Environment and Development: Global Challenge, International Response.* Tucson: University of Arizona Press, 1990.

Episcopal Pastoral Letter. "Our Relationship with Nature." *Latin American Documentation,* vol. 18, 1987, pp. 12–22.

Ette, A. and R. Waller. "The Anomaly of a Christian Ecology." *Ecologist Quarterly,* Summer 1978, pp. 144–48.

Evans, Bernard F. and Gregory D. Cusack, eds. *Theology of the Land.* Collegeville, Minn.: The

Liturgical Press, 1987.

Evans, J. "Use and Abuse of Tropical Forests." *Science and Christian Belief,* vol. 2, no. 2, 1990, pp. 141–44.

Evdokimov, Paul. "Nature." *Scottish Journal of Theology,* March 1965, pp. 1–22.

Everett, W. *Land Ethics: Toward a Covenantal Model.* Newton Centre, Mass.: The American Society of Christian Ethics, 1979.

Fackre, Gabriel. "Ecology and Theology." *Religion in Life,* Summer 1971, pp. 210–24.

Fagley, Richard. *The Population Explosion and Christian Responsibility.* New York: Oxford University Press, 1960.

Falcke, Heino. "Confronting Threats to Peace and Survival: Theological Aspects." *Ecumenical Review,* January 1984, pp. 33–42.

———. "Biblical Aspects of the Process of Mutual Commitment." *Ecumenical Review,* July 1986, pp. 257–64.

———. "The Integrity of Creation." *One World,* April 1987, pp. 15–18.

Faramelli, Norman J. "Ecological Responsibility and Economic Justice: The Perilous Links between Ecology and Poverty." *Andover Newton Quarterly,* December 1970, pp. 81–93.

———. *Technetics: Christian Mission in an Age of Technology.* New York: Friendship Press, 1971.

———. "Ecological Responsibility and Church Investments." *Church and Society,* March–April 1972, pp. 23–55.

———. "Toying with the Environment and the Poor: A Report on the Stockholm Environmental Conference." *Environmental Affairs,* Winter 1972, pp. 469–86.

———. "Urban Ecology: Basis for a New Alliance." *New World Outlook,* July-August 1972, pp. 9–15.

———. "The Role of the Church in Eco-Justice: A JSAC Working Paper." *Church and Society,* November-December 1973, pp. 4–15.

———, and Charles Powers. "Environmental Ethics: Questions of Social Justice." *Encyclopedia of Bioethics,* ed. Warren T. Reich. New York: Free Press, 1978. vol. 1, pp. 388–92.

Faricy, Robert. *Wind and Sea Obey Him.* London: SCM Press, 1982.

Ferré, Frederick. *Shaping the Future: Resources for the Post-Modern World.* New York: Harper and Row, 1976.

———. "Religious World Modeling and Postmodern Science." *Journal of Religion,* July 1982, pp. 261–71.

———. "The Integrity of Creation." *Empirical Theology,* ed. Randolph Crump Miller. Birming-ham, Ala.: Religious Education Press, 1992.

———. *Hellfire and Lightning Rods: Liberating Science, Technology, and Religion.* Maryknoll, N.Y.: Orbis Press, 1993.

Fox, Matthew. *Western Spirituality: Historical Roots, Ecumenical Roots.* Notre Dame, Ind.: Fides/Claretian, 1979.

———. *Original Blessing: A Primer in Creation Spirituality.* Santa Fe: Bear and Co., 1983.

———. *The Coming of the Cosmic Christ.* San Francisco: Harper and Row, 1988.

Fretheim, Terrence E. *Creation, Fall and Flood.* Minneapolis: Augsburg, 1969.

Freudenberger, C. Dean and Paul Minus. *Christian Responsibility in a Hungry World.* Nashville: Abingdon Press, 1975.

———. *The Gift of Land.* Los Angeles: Franciscan Communications, 1981.

———. "Resource Abuse: 'The Land Does Not Lie'." *The Causes of World Hunger,* ed. W. J. Byron. New York: Paulist Press, 1982, pp. 90–105.

———. *Food for Tomorrow?* Minneapolis: Augsburg, 1984.

———. *Global Dustbowl: Can We Stop the Destruction of the Land before It's Too Late?* Minneapolis: Augsburg, 1990.

Fritsch, Albert J. *A Theology of the Earth.* Washington: CLB Publishers, 1972.

———, and Science Action Coalition. *Environmental Ethics: Choices for Concerned Citizens.* Garden City, NY: Anchor Press/Doubleday, 1980.

————. *Renew the Face of the Earth.* Chicago: Loyola University Press, 1987.

Froehlich, Karl F. "Ecology of Creation." *Theology Today,* October 1970, pp. 263–76.

Furuya, Keiichi. "Faith, Science and the Future: MIT Conference Report." *Japan Christian Quarterly,* Spring 1980, pages 73–82.

Gambell, Ray. "Whaling: A Christian Position." *Science and Christian Belief,* April 1990, pp. 15–24.

Garriott, Charlie. "A Theology for All My Relatives: Are You at Peace with Your Nonhuman Relatives in Creation?" *Other Side,* January 1983, pp. 16–19.

Gelderloos, Orin G. *Eco-Theology.* Glasgow: Wild Goose Publications, 1992.

Ghosh, Sailendranath. "Understanding the Integrity of Variegated Creation for Survival." *Religion and Society* (Bangalore), June 1990, pp. 35–45.

Gibbs, John G. *Creation and Redemption: A Study in Pauline Theology.* Leiden: E. J. Brill, 1971.

————. "Pauline Cosmic Christology and Ecological Crisis." *Journal of Biblical Literature,* December 1971, pp. 466–79.

Gibson, William E. "Ecojustice: Burning Word: Heilbroner and Jeremiah to the Church." *Foundations,* October-December 1977, pp. 318–28.

————. "Sustainable Security: Peace Education and Ecological/Economic Responsibility." *Moving Toward Shalom: Essays in Memory of John T. Conner,* ed. Dieter Hessel. Nyack, N.Y.: Fellowship of Reconciliation, 1987.

————. "An Order in Crisis, and the Declaration of New Things." *Reformed Faith and Economics,* ed. R. L. Stivers. Lanham, Md.: University Press of America, 1988, pp. 145–70.

Gilbert, T. L. "Nature, Technology, and Theology." *Zygon,* October 1992, pp. 203–10.

Gilkey, Langdon. *Reaping the Whirlwind: A Christian Interpretation of History.* New York: Seabury Press, 1976.

————. *Nature, Reality, and the Sacred.* Minneapolis: Fortress Press, 1993.

————. "Nature as the Image of God: Signs of the Sacred." *Theology Today,* April 1994, pp. 127–41.

Gill, J. H. "The Ethics of Environment." *Reformed Journal,* May 1978, pp. 18–21.

Gittens, Anthony J. "Toward an Integral Spirituality: Embodiment, Ecology, and Experience of God." *Common Journey, Different Paths,* ed. Susan Rakorzy. Maryknoll, N.Y.: Orbis Press, 1992, pp. 44–54.

————. "Ecology and World Poverty: A Christian Response." *Spirituality Today,* vol. 38, 1986, pp. 19–30.

Given, David R. "Biblical Aspects of Conservation—Rediscovering the Greenness in Christianity." *CBRF Journal,* March 1991. pp. 23–31.

Gomes, Peter J. "Critique of W. E. Gibson's 'Ecojustice: Burning Word'." *Foundations,* October-December 1977, pp. 329–32.

Goodwin, Ellie. "A Country of Ostriches." *Christianity and Crisis,* 22 June 1992, pp. 224–26.

Gore, Albert J. "Earth in the Balance." *Christian Century,* 18 April 1992, pp. 373–74.

————. *Earth in the Balance.* New York: Penguin, 1992.

Gosling, David. "Towards a Credible Ecumenical Theology of Nature." *Ecumenical Review,* July 1986, pp. 322–31,

Gowan, Donald E. "Genesis and Ecology: Does 'Subdue' Mean 'Plunder'?" *Christian Century,* October 7, 1970, pp. 1188–91.

————, and M. Schumaker. *Genesis and Ecology: An Exchange.* Kingston, Ont.: Queen's Theological College, 1973.

————. "The Fall and Redemption of the Material World in Apocalyptic Literature." *Horizons in Biblical Theology,* December 1985, pp. 83–103.

Granberg-Michaelson, Wesley. "At the Dawn of the New Creation: A Theology of the Environment." *Sojourners,* November 1981, pp. 13–16.

————. "Earthkeeping: A Theology for Global Sanctification." *Sojourners,* October 1982, pp. 21–24.

————. "The Promise of God's Reign: the Church's Role in the World's Future." *Sojourners,*

June–July 1984, pp. 16–19.

———. *A Worldly Spirituality: The Call to Redeem Life on Earth.* San Francisco: Harper and Row, 1984.

———, ed. *Tending the Garden: Essays on the Gospel and the Earth.* Grand Rapids, Mich.: Wm. B. Eerdmans, 1987.

———. *Ecology and Life: Accepting Our Environmental Responsibility.* Waco, Tex.: Word Books, 1988.

———. *Redeeming the Creation: The Rio Summit: Challenges for the Churches.* Geneva: World Council of Churches, 1992.

Gray, Elizabeth Dodson. *Why the Green Nigger? Re-Mything Genesis.* Wesllesley, Mass.: Roundtable Press, 1979 (republished as *Green Paradise Lost* in 1982).

Greeley, Andrew M. "Religion in Attitudes toward the Environment." *Journal for the Scientific Study of Religion,* March 1993, pp. 19–28.

Gregorios, Paulos Mar. *The Human Presence: An Orthodox View of Nature.* Geneva: World Council of Churches, 1978.

Griffin, David Ray. "Whitehead's Contribution to a Theology of Nature." *Bucknell Review,* Winter 1972, pp. 3–24.

———. "A Process Theology of Creation." *Mid-Stream,* Fall–Winter 1973/74, pp. 48–70.

———. "A New Vision of Nature." *Encounter,* Spring 1974, pp. 95–107.

———, ed. *The Reenchantment of Science: Postmodern Proposals.* Albany: State University of New York Press, 1988.

———, ed. *Spirituality and Society: Postmodern Visions.* Albany: State University of New York Press, 1988.

———. *God and Religion in the Postmodern World: Essays in Postmodern Theology.* Albany: State University of New York Press, 1989.

———, ed. *Sacred Interconnections: Postmodern Spirituality, Political Economy, and Art.* Albany: State University of New York Press, 1990.

———. "Green Spirituality: A Postmodern Convergence of Science and Religion." *Journal of Theology: United Theological Seminary,* 1992, pp. 5–21.

Grove-White, Robin. "The Christian 'Person' and Environmental Concerns." *Studies in Christian Ethics,* vol. 2, 1992, pp. 1–17.

Gulick, Walter B. "The Bible and Ecological Spirituality." *Theology Today,* July 1992, pp. 182–94.

Guroian, Vegen. "Toward Ecology as an Ecclesial Event: Orthodox Theology and Ethics." *Communio* (U.S.), Spring 1991, pp. 89–110.

Gustafson, James M. "Interdependence, Finitude and Sin: Reflections on Scarcity." *Journal of Religion,* April 1977, pp. 156–68.

———. *Ethics from a Theocentric Perspective,* 2 vols. Chicago: University of Chicago Press, 1981–84.

———. "Ethical Issues in the Human Future," *Human Adaptation: A Biocultural Odyssey,* ed. Donald J. Ortner. Washington: Smithsonian Press, 1983, pp. 491–516.

———. *A Sense of the Divine: The Natural Environment from a Theocentric Perspective.* Cleveland: Pilgrim Press, 1994.

Hadsell, Heidi. "Creation Theology and the Doing of Ethics." *Horizons of Biblical Theology,* December 1992, pp. 93–111.

Hall, Douglas John. *The Steward: A Biblical Symbol Come of Age.* New York: Friendship Press, 1982.

———. *Christian Mission: The Stewardship of Life in the Kingdom of Death.* New York: Friendship Press, 1985.

———. *Imaging God: Dominion as Stewardship.* Grand Rapids, Mich.: Wm. B. Eerdmans, 1987.

Hallman, David G. *Caring for Creation: The Environmental Crisis—A Canadian Christian Call to Action.* Winfield, B.C.: Wood Lake Books, 1989.

———. *A Place in Creation: Ecological Visions in Science, Religion and Economics.* Toronto:

United Church Publishing House, 1992.

————, ed. *Ecotheology: Insights from South and North.* New York: World Council of Churches, 1994. (Also published by Orbis Press.)

Halkes, Catherine J. M. *Christian Feminism and the Renewal of the Earth.* London: SPCK, 1991.

Hamilton, Michael, ed. *This Little Planet.* New York: Scribner's, 1969.

Harakas, S. S. "The Integrity of Creation and Ethics." *St. Vladimir's Theological Quarterly,* 1 November 1988, pp. 27–42.

Hardin, Garrett. "Ecology and the Death of Providence." *Zygon,* March 1980, pp. 57–69.

Hargrove, Eugene C. *Foundations of Environmental Ethics.* Englewood Cliffs: Prentice Hall, 1989.

————, ed. *Religion and Environmental Crisis.* Athens: University of Georgia Press, 1986.

Harrison, Beverly W., Robert L. Stivers, and Ronald H. Stone, eds. *The Public Vocation of Christian Ethics.* New York: Pilgrim Press, 1986.

Hart, John. *The Spirit of the Earth.* New York/Ramsey, N.J.: Paulist Press, 1984.

Hartman, Olov. "Christ and the Garden." *Lutheran Forum,* February 1972, pp. 26–28.

Haught, John F. *The Promise of Nature: Ecology and Cosmic Purpose.* New York/Mahwah, N.J.: Paulist Press, 1993.

————. "Theology and the Environmental Crisis." *Minding the Times,* ed. William J. O'Brien. Washington: Georgetown University Press, 1992, pp. 37–58.

Hayes, Zachry. *What Are They Saying About Creation?* Ramsey, N.J.: Paulist Press, 1980.

Hefner, Philip J. "The Politics and Ontology of Nature and Grace." *Journal of Religion,* April 1974, pp. 138–53.

Heinegg, Peter. "Ecology and the Fall." *Christian Century,* May 12, 1976, pp. 464–66.

Heiss, Richard L. and Noel F. McInnis. *Can Man Care for the Earth?* Nashville: Abingdon Press, 1971.

Helgeland, John. "Land and Eschatology." *Dialog,* Summer 1980, pp. 186–92.

Hendry, George S. "The Eclipse of Creation." *Theology Today,* January 1972, pp. 406–25.

————. *Theology of Nature.* Philadelphia: Westminster Press, 1980.

Henry, Carl F. H. "Stewardship of the Environment." *Applying the Scriptures: Papers from ICBI Summit III,* ed. K. S. Kanzer. Grand Rapids, Mich.: Zondervan, 1987, pp. 473–88.

Hessel, Dieter T., ed. *Beyond Survival: Bread and Justice in Christian Perspective.* New York: Friendship Press, 1977.

————, ed. *Energy Ethics: A Christian Response.* New York: Friendship Press, 1979.

————, and G. Wilson. *Congregational Lifestyle Changes for the Lean Years.* New York: United Presbyterian Program Agency, 1981.

————, ed. *For Creation's Sake: Preaching, Ecology and Justice.* Philadelphia: Geneva Press, 1985.

————, ed. *After Nature's Revolt: Eco-Justice and Theology.* Minneapolis: Fortress Press, 1992.

Hiers, Richard H. "Ecology, Biblical Theology, and Methodology: Biblical Perspectives on the Environment." *Zygon,* March 1984, pp. 43–59.

Hoehler, Harry H. and Judith Hoehler. "The Bible, Stewardship and the Care of the Earth." *Unitarian Universalist Christian,* Spring/Summer 1993, pp. 59–67.

Hough, Joseph C. Jr. "Land and People: The Eco-Justice Connection." *Christian Century,* October 1, 1980, pages 910–14.

————. "The Care of the Earth: The Moral Basis for Land Conservation." *Quarterly Review,* Summer 1981, pp. 3–22.

Houston, J. M. "The Environmental Movement: Five Causes of Confusion." *Christianity Today,* 15 September 1972, pp. 1131–32.

Hundertmark, Nadine. *Pro-Earth.* New York: Friendship Press, 1985.

Hurst, J. S. "Towards a Theology of Conservation." *Theology,* April 1972, pp. 197–205.

Ice, J. L. "Ecological Crisis: Radical Monotheism and Ethical Pantheism." *Religion in Life,* Summer 1975, pp. 203–211.

Imsland, D. *Celebrate the Earth.* Minneapolis: Augsburg, 1971.

Innes, K. *Caring for the Earth: The Environment, Christians, and the Church.* Bramcote, Nottinghamshire, GB: Grove Books, 1987.

Institute for Ecumenical Research. "Theology of Creation—Contributions and Deficits of Our Confessional Traditions." *Ecumenical Review,* April 1984, pp. 204–213.

International Consultation on Simple Lifestyle. *An Evangelical Commitment to Simple Lifestyle.* Philadelphia: Theology and Education Group and the World Evangelical Fellowship's Theological Commission Unit on Ethics and Society, 1980.

Jackson, Wes. *Altars of Unhewn Stone: Science and Nature.* San Francisco: North Point Press, 1987.

————, Wendell Berry, and B. Coleman. *Meeting the Expectations of the Land: Essays in Sustainable Agriculture and Stewardship.* San Francisco: North Point Press, 1984.

Janecko, Benedict. "Ecology, Nature and the Psalms." *Psalms and Other Studies,* ed. Jack C. Knight and Lawrence A. Sinclair. Natosha, Wis.: Natosha House Seminary, 1990, pp. 96–108.

Jegen, Mary Evelyn and C. W. Tilberg. *The Human Crisis in Ecology.* New York: Board of Social Ministry, Lutheran Church in America, 1972.

———— and Bruno V. Manno, eds. *The Earth is the Lord's: Essays on Stewardship.* New York: Paulist Press, 1978.

Jones, Donald L. "Corporateness and the Ecological Consciousness." *Religion in Life,* Summer 1971, pp. 203–09.

Joranson, Philip N. and Alan C. Anderson, eds. *Religious Reconstruction for the Environmental Future.* South Coventry, Conn.: Faith-Man-Nature Group, 1973.

————. "The Faith-Man-Nature Group and a Religious Environmental Ethic." *Zygon,* June 1977, pp. 175–79.

————, and Ken Butigan, eds. *Cry of the Environment: Rebuilding the Christian Creation Tradition.* Santa Fe: Bear and Company, 1984.

Kahl, Brigette. "Human Culture and the Integrity of Creation Biblical Reflections on Genesis 1–11." *Ecumenical Review,* April 1987, pp. 128–37.

Kaiser, Christopher B. "Faith and Science and the WCC." *Reformed World,* vol. 35, no. 8, 1979, pp. 330–36.

Kaufman, Gordon. "A Problem for Theology: The Concept of Nature." *Harvard Theological Review,* July 1972, pp. 337–66.

————. "An Ecological Ethic." Chap. 14 in *In Face of Mystery: A Constructive Theology.* Cambridge, Mass.: Harvard University Press, 1993.

Kay, Jeanne. "Concepts of Nature in the Hebrew Bible." *Environmental Ethics,* Winter 1988, pp. 309–27.

Kerr, Hugh T. "Ecosystems and Systematics." *Theology Today,* April 1972, pp. 104–19.

Khalil, Issa J. "Ecological Crisis: An Eastern Christian Perspective." *St. Vladimir's Theological Quarterly,* 4 November 1978, pp. 193–211.

Kim, Yong Bock. "The Sustainable Society: An Asian Perspective." *Ecumenical Review,* April 1979, pp. 169–78.

King, P. "Global Stewardship." *The Changing World,* ed. B. Kaye. Glasgow: Collins, 1977.

King, R. H. "Ecological Motif in the Theology of H. Richard Niebuhr." *Journal of the American Academy of Religion,* June 1974, pp. 339–43.

King, Sallie and Steven Kraft. "Process Metaphysics and Minimalism: Implications for Public Policy." *Environmental Ethics,* Spring 1991, pp. 23–47.

Kingston, A. Richard. "Christian Duty and Animal Welfare." *Theology,* June 1968, pp. 250–56.

Kirkwood, Karen. "Flush Toilets and Justice: The Environmental Masquerade." *Other Side,* January–February 1992, pp. 28–29.

Kirshenmann, Frederick. "Rediscovering American Agriculture." *Word and World,* Summer 1993, pp. 294–303.

Klink, W. H. "Environmental Concerns and the Need for a New Image of Man." *Zygon,* December 1974, pp. 300–10.

Klotz, J. W. *Ecology Crisis: God's Creation and Man's Pollution.* St. Louis: Concordia, 1971.

Knight, Peter. *The Politics of Conservation: Christians and the Good Earth.* Alexandria, Va.: The Faith-Man-Nature Group, 1967.

Krueger, Frederick W., ed. *Christian Ecology: Building an Environmental Ethic for the Twenty-First Century.* San Francisco: North American Conference of Christian Ecologists, 1988.

LaBar, Martin. "Message to Polluters from the Bible." *Christianity Today,* 26 July 1974, pp. 1186–90.

Land, Richard and Louis Moore, eds. *The Earth is the Lord's: Christians and the Environment.* Nashville: Broadman Press, 1992.

Laszlo, Ervin. "Human Survival: The Responsibility of Science and Religion." *Zygon,* December 1991, pp. 547–54.

Lechte, R. E. "Partnerships for Ecological Well-being." *Ecumenical Review,* April 1990, pp. 157–61.

Leckie, Joe L. *God's Green Gifts: Renewable Energy Sources.* Carberry, Great Britian: Handsel Press, 1992.

Lilburne, Geoffrey R. *A Sense of Place.* Nashville: Abingdon Press, 1989.

Limburg, James. "What Does It Mean to 'Have Dominion over the Earth'?" *Dialog,* Summer 1971, pp. 221–23.

———. *A Good Land.* Minneapolis: Augsburg, 1981.

Limouris, Gennadios. "Integrity of Creation and Earth." *Mid-Mid-Stream,* July 1989, pp. 249–62.

———, ed. *Justice, Peace and the Integrity of Creation: Insights from Orthodoxy.* Geneva: World Council of Churches, 1990.

Lindqvist, Matti. *Economic Growth and the Quality of Life: An Analysis of the Debate within the World Council of Churches 1966-1974.* Helsinki: Finnish Society for Missiology and Ecumenics, 1975.

Lindsell, Harold. "Lord's Day and Natural Resources." *Christianity Today,* 7 May 1976, pp. 8–12.

Linzey, Andrew. *Animal Rights: A Christian Assessment of Man's Treatment of Animals.* London: SCM Press, 1976.

———. "The Place of Animals in Creation: A Christian View." *Animal Sacrifice: Religious Perspectives on the Use of Animals in Science,* ed. Tom Regan. Philadelphia: Temple University Press, 1986.

———. *Christianity and the Rights of Animals.* New York: Crossroad, 1987.

———, and Tom Regan, eds. *Animals and Christianity: A Book of Readings.* New York: Crossroad, 1988.

———, eds. *Love the Animals: Meditations and Prayers.* New York: Crossroad, 1989.

———, ed. *Cruelty and Christian Conscience: Bishops Say No to Fur.* Nottingham, Great Britian: Lynx Educational Trust, 1992.

———. "Animal Rights: A Reply to Barclay." *Science and Christian Beliefs,* April 1973, pp. 47–51.

———. "Liberation Theology and the Oppression of Animals." *Scottish Journal of Theology,* vol. 46, no. 4, 1993, pp. 507–25.

Livingston, James C. "The Ecological Challenge to Christian Ethics." *Christian Century,* 1 December 1971, pp. 409–12.

Lochman, Jan M. "Trends in the Ecumenical Dialogue on Faith and Science." *Journal of Ecumenical Studies,* Summer 1980, pp. 432–44.

Locke, John W. "Ministry in an Endangered World." *Lexington Theological Quarterly,* January 1991, pp. 25–29.

Lonergan, Anne and Caroline Richards, ed. *Thomas Berry and the New Cosmology.* Mystic, Conn.: Twenty-Third Publications, 1987.

Longacre, D. J. *Living More with Less.* Scottdale, Pa.: Herald Press, 1980.

Longwood, Merle. "Toward an Environmental Ethic." *That They May Live: Theological Reflections on the Quality of Life,* ed. George Devine. Staten Island, N.Y.: Alba House, 1972, pp. 47–68.

————. "Common Good: An Ethical Framework for Evaluating Environmental Issues." *Theological Studies,* September 1973, pp. 468–80.

Lonning, Per. *Creation—An Ecumenical Challenge: Reflections Issuing from a Study by the Institute for Ecumenical Research, Strasbourg, France.* Macon, Ga.: Mercer University Press, 1989.

Lowery, Richard H. "Sabbath and Survival: Abundance and Self-Restraint in a Culture of Excess." *Encounter,* Spring 1993, pp. 143–67.

Lutz, C. P., ed. *Farming the Lord's Land: Christian Perspectives on American Agriculture.* Minneapolis: Augsburg, 1980.

Lutz, P. E. and Paul Santmire. *Ecological Renewal.* Philadelphia: Confrontation Books, 1972.

Macquarrie, John. "Creation and Environment." *Expository Times,* October 1971, pp. 4–9.

————. "The Idea of a Theology of Nature." *Union Seminary Quarterly Review,* Winter–Summer, 1975, pp. 69–75.

Marietta, D.E. "Relgious Models and Ecological Decision Making." *Zygon,* June 1977, pp. 151–66.

Marshall, Paul. "Does the Creation Have Rights?" *Studies in Christian Ethics,* vol. 2, 1993, pp. 31–49.

Martin, Charles W. "Ecology and Theology." *Living Church,* November 1970, pp. 14–16.

Massey, Marshall. *The Defense of the Peaceable Kingdom.* Oakland: Pacific Yearly Meeting, Religious Society of Friends, 1985.

McClellan, Monique. "On the Way to Rio: Churches and the Earth Summit." *One World,* October 1991, pp. 10–12.

McCormick, R. A. "Toward an Ethics of Ecology." *Theological Studies,* March 1971, pp. 97–107.

McCoy, Jerry D. "Towards a Theology of Nature." *Encounter,* Summer 1985, pp. 213–28.

McDaniel, Jay B. "Christian Spirituality as Openness to Fellow Creatures." *Environmental Ethics,* Spring 1986, pp. 33–46.

————. "Christianity and the Pursuit of Wealth." *Anglican Theological Review,* October 1987, pp. 349–61.

————. "Land Ethics, Animal Rights, and Process Theology." *Process Studies,* Summer 1988, pp. 88–102.

————. *Of God and Pelicans: A Theology of Reverence for Life.* Louisville: Westminster/John Knox, 1989.

————. *Earth, Sky, Gods, and Mortals: Developing an Ecological Christianity.* Mystic, Conn.: Twenty-Third Publications, 1990.

————. "Howling with the Wolves: Paul Winter's Earth Jazz." *Black Sacred Music,* Spring 1992, pp. 170–76.

McDonagh, Sean. *To Care for the Earth: A Call to a New Theology.* London: Chapman, 1986.

————. *The Greening of the Church.* Maryknoll, N.Y.: Orbis Press, 1990.

McFague, Sally. *Models of God: Theology for an Ecological, Nuclear Age.* Philadelphia: Fortress Press, 1987.

————. "The Theologian as Advocate." *Theological Education, Spring* 1989, pp. 79–97.

————. *The Body of God: An Ecological Theology.* Minneapolis: Fortress Press, 1993.

McIntyre, J. "The Theological Dimension of the Ecological Problem." *Scottish Journal of Religious Studies,* Autumn 1982, pp. 83–96.

McPherson, James. "Toward an Ecological Theology." *Expository Times,* May 1986, pp. 236–40.

————. "Ecumenical Discussion of the Environment 1966-1987." *Modern Theology,* July 1991, pp. 363–71.

Means, Richard L. "Man and Nature: The Theological Vacuum." *Christian Century,* 1 May 1968, pp. 579–81.

Meland, Bernard E. "Grace: a Dimension within Nature." *Journal of Religion,* April 1974, pp. 119–37.

Mellert, Robert. "Models and Metanoia." *Proceedings of the Catholic Philosophical Association,* 1973, pp. 142–52.

Mertens, H. "The Doctrine of Creation in Ecological Perspective." *Louvain Studies,* Spring 1987, pp. 83–88.

Metz, Johann B. and Edward Schillebeeckx, eds. *No Heaven without Earth.* Philadelphia: Trinity Press, 1991.

Meyer, Art and Jocelle Meyer. *Earth-Keepers: Environmental Perspectives on Hunger, Poverty, and Injustice.* Scottdale, Pa.: Herald Press, 1991.

Migliore, Daniel L. "The Ecological Crisis and the Doctrine of Creation." *Princeton Seminary Bulletin,* vol. 12, no. 3, 1991, pp. 266–82.

Mitcham, Carl and Jim Grote, eds. *Theology and Technology: Essays in Christian Analysis and Exegesis.* Lanham, Md.: University Press of America, 1984.

Moberly, R. W. "Did the Serpent Get It Right?" *Journal of Theological Studies,* April 1988, pp. 1–27.

Moltmann, Juergen. "Creation as an Open System." Chap. 8 in *The Future of Creation,* trans. Margaret Kohl. Philadelphia: Fortress Press, 1979, pp. 115–27.

———. *God in Creation: A New Theology of Creation and the Spirit of God,* trans. Margaret Kohl. San Francisco: Harper and Row, 1985.

———. "The Ecological Crisis: Peace with Nature?" *Scottish Journal of Religious Studies,* Spring 1988, pp. 5–18.

Montefiore, Hugh. *Can Man Survive?* London: Collins, 1970.

———, ed. *Man and Nature.* London: Collins, 1975.

———. "Religion and the Politics of the Environment." *Religion in Public Life,* ed. Dan Cohn-Sherbok and David McLellan. New York: St. Martin's Press, 1992, pp. 51–63.

Moore, Arthur J. "Meeting on Science and Faith Debates Ethics and Technology." *Christianity and Crisis,* 15 October 1979, pp. 244–47.

Moore, Peter D. "The Exploitation of Forests." *Science and Christian Belief,* October 1990, pp. 131–40.

Morikawa, Jitsuo. "Evangelistic Lifestyle in an Eco-Just Universe." *Foundations,* July–September 1975, pp. 272–81.

Morton, J. P. "Listen to the Land." *Christianity and Crisis,* 4 February 1980, pp. 10–12.

Moss, Rowland P. "Environmental Problems and the Christian Ethic." *Horizons of Science: Christian Scholars Speak Out,* ed. Carl F. H. Henry. San Francisco: Harper and Row, 1978, pp. 63–86.

———. *The Earth in Our Hands.* London: InterVarsity Press, 1982.

Moule, C. F. D. *Man and Nature in the New Testament: Some Reflections on Biblical Ecology.* Philadelphia: Fortress Press, 1967.

Muray, Leslie A. "The Hungarian 'Blues,' North American Process Philosophy, and Environmental Ethics." *Encounter,* Summer 1972, pp. 231–46.

Murphey, Charles M. *At Home on Earth: Foundations for a Catholic Ethic of the Environment.* New York: Crossroad/Continuum, 1989.

Nash, James A. *Loving Nature: Ecological Integrity and Christian Responsibility.* Nashville: Abingdon Press, 1991.

———. "Ethical Concerns for the Global-Warming Debate." *Christian Century,* 26 August–2 September 1992, pp. 773–76.

Nash, R. F. "The Greening of Religion." Chap. 4 in *The Rights of Nature: A History of Environmental Ethics.* Madison, Wis.: University of Wisconsin Press, 1989.

Navone, John. "Christian Responsibility for the Environment." *American Ecclesiastical Review,* December 1975, pp. 681–89.

Neuhaus, Richard John. *In Defense of People: Ecology and the Seduction of Radicalism.* New York: Macmillan, 1971.

———. "In Defense of People: A Thesis Revisited," *Environmental Quality and Social Justice in Urban America,* ed. James Noel Smith. Washington: The Conservation Foundation, 1974, pp. 59–72.

Niles, D. Preman. *Resisting the Threats to Life: Covenanting for Justice, Peace and the Integrity of Creation.* Geneva: WCC Publications, 1989.

————. *Between the Flood and the Rainbow: Interpreting the Conciliar Process of Mutual Commitment (Covenant) to Justice, Peace and the Integrity of Creation.* Geneva: WCC Publications, 1992.

Nurnberger, Klaus, ed. *Ecology and Christian Ethics in a Semi-industrialized and Polarised Society.* Pretoria: University of South Africa, 1987.

Oates, David. "Whose is the Earth?" *Other Side,* August 1983, pp. 14–17.

Obayashi, Hiroshi. "Nature and Historicization: A Theological Reflection on Ecology." *CrossCurrents,* Summer 1973, pp. 140–52.

O'Brien, James F. "Teilhard's View of Nature and Some Implications for Environmental Ethics." *Environmental Ethics,* Winter 1988, pp. 329–46.

Oelschlaeger, Max. *Caring for Creation: An Ecumenical Approach to the Environmental Crisis.* New Haven: Yale University Press, 1994.

Ogden, Schubert M. "Prolegomena to a Christian Theology of Nature." *A Rational Faith: Essays in Honor of Levi A. Olan,* ed. Jack Bemporad. New York: KTAV Publishing House, 1977, pp. 125–36.

————. "Subtler Forms of Bondage and Liberation." Chap. 4 of *Faith and Freedom.* Nashville: Abingdon Press, 1979.

O'Gorman, Kathleen Ann. "Toward the Cultivation of Ecological Spirituality." *Religious Education,* Fall 1992, pp. 606–18.

Oliver, Harold H. "The Neglect and Recovery of Nature in 20th Century Protestant Thought." *Journal of the American Academy of Religion,* Fall 1992, pp. 379–404.

Olsen, Lani J. "Five Years after Science Conference: Three Stories." *One World,* March 1984, pp. 8–9.

O'Mahoney, Donald, "International Debt and Ecological Connections." *SEDOS Bulletin,* 15 December 1992, pp. 325–49.

Owens, Owen D. *Stones into Bread: What does the Bible Say about Feeding the Hungry Today?* Valley Forge, Pa.: Judson Press, 1977.

————. *Living Waters: How to Save Your Local Stream.* New Brunswick, N.J.: Rutgers University Press, 1993.

Paddock, Joe, Nancy Paddock, and Carol Bly. "Dust to Dust: Land in the Jewish and Christian Traditions." Chap. 8 in *Soil and Survival: Land Stewardship and the Future of American Agriculture.* San Francisco: Sierra Club Books, 1986.

Palmer, Martin. "The Ecological Crisis and Creation Theology." *Interpreting the Universe as Creation,* ed. Vincent Bruemmer. Kampen, Netherlands: Kok Pharaos, 1991, pp. 132–46.

Paradise, Scott. "Visions of the Good Society and the Energy Debate." *Anglican Theological Review,* January–February 1970, pp. 14–23.

Parmar, Samuel L. "The Limits-to-Growth Debate in Asian Perspective." *Ecumenical Review,* January 1974, pp. 33–52.

Passmore, John. *Man's Responsibility for Nature: Ecological Problems and Western Traditions.* New York: Scribner's, 1974; 2d ed., London: Duckworth, 1980.

Paternoster, M. *Man: The World's High Priest: An Ecological Approach.* Oxford: Sisters of the Love of God, 1976.

Peacocke, A. R. *Creation and the World of Science.* Oxford: Oxford University Press, 1979.

Peck, Jane Cary. "Report on WCC Conference." *Andover Newton Quarterly,* March 1980, pp. 191–98.

Peerman, Dean. "Gertrude Blom: Prophet Crying *for* a Wilderness." *Christian Century,* 11 December 985, pp. 1146–50.

Perdue, Leo G. *Wisdom and Creation: The Theology of Wisdom Literature.* Nashville: Abingdon Press, 1992.

Pinches, Charles and Jay B. McDaniel, eds. *Good News for Animals?* Maryknoll, N.Y.: Orbis Press, 1993.

Pitcher, W. Alvin. *Listen to the Crying of the Earth: Cultivating Creation Communities.*

Cleveland: Pilgrim Press, 1993.

Pobee, John. *Religion, Morality, Population Dynamics.* Legon, Ghana: Population Dynamics Program, University of Ghana, 1977.

———. "Creation Faith and Responsibility for the World." *Journal of Theology for Southern Africa,* March 1985, pp. 16–26.

Pope John Paul II. *Peace with God the Creator—Peace with All of Creation.* Vatican City: Libreria Editrice Vatican, 1990.

Prance, Ghillean T. "Appropriate Technology and Christian Belief: A Case Study of Amazonia." *Science and Christian Belief,* April 1993, pp. 5–17.

Presbyterian Eco-Justice Task Force. *Keeping and Healing the Creation.* Louisville: Committee on Social Witness Policy, Presbyterian Church (USA), 1989.

Preston, R. H. "The Question of a Just, Participatory, and Sustainable Society." *Bulletin of the John Rylands University Library of Manchester,* Autumn 1980, pp. 95–117.

Primavesi, Anne. "The Part for the Whole: An Ecofeminist Enquiry." *Theology,* September-October 1990, pp. 355–62.

———. *From Apocalypse to Genesis: Ecology, Feminism and Christianity.* Kent, Great Britian: Burnes and Oates, 1991.

Pritchard, Colin. "Science, Faith and the Vision of a New Society." *Theology,* September 1977, pp. 331–40.

Quinn, Frederick. *That We May Heal the Earth: A Theology of Ecology.* Nashville: Upper Room Books, 1994.

Rae, Eleanor. *Women, the Earth, the Divine.* Maryknoll, N.Y.: Orbis Press, 1994.

Rajotte, F. "Creationist Theology at the W.C.C." *Ecumenist,* September-October 1988, pp. 85–90.

Rakestraw, Robert V. "The Contribution of John Wesley toward an Ethics of Nature." *Drew Gateway,* Spring 1986, pp. 14–25.

Rappaport, Roy A. *Ecology, Meaning, and Religion.* Richmond, Calif.: North Atlantic Books, 1979.

Rasmussen, Larry. "The Future Isn't What It Used to Be: 'Limits to Growth' and Christian Ethics." *Lutheran Quarterly,* May 1975, pp. 101–11.

———. "The Bishops and the Economy: Three Appraisals; III. On Creation, On Growth." *Christianity and Crisis,* November 1985, pp. 473–76.

———. "The Planetary Environment: Challenge on Every Front." *Theology and Public Policy,* Summer 1990, pp. 3–14.

———. "Toward an Earth Charter." *Christian Century,* 23 October 1991, pp. 964–67.

———. "Honoring Creation's Integrity: The Ecocrisis." *Christianity and Crisis,* 18 November 1991, pp. 354–58.

———. "Ecocrisis and Theology's Quest: Today's Theologies Must Include a Cosmology and Ethic Worthy of the Name." *Christianity and Crisis,* 16 March 1992, pp. 83–87.

Regenstein, Lewis G. *Replenish the Earth.* New York: Crossroad, 1991.

Reidel, C. H. "Christianity and the Environmental Crisis." *Christianity Today,* 23 April 1971, pp. 684–88.

Rendtorff, Rolf. "'Subdue the Earth': Man and Nature in the Old Testament." *Theology Digest,* Fall 1979, pp. 213–16.

Reuss, Carl F. "Towards More Justice: A Review of the WCC Program Emphasis." *Ecumenical Review,* April 1979, pp. 163–68.

Rhoads, David. "The Role of the Church in the Care of the Earth." *Currents in Theology and Mission,* December 1991, pp. 406–14.

Richardson, C. C. "A Christian Approach to Ecology." *Religion in Life,* Winter 1972, pp. 462–79.

Rifkin, Jeremy, with Ted Howard. *The Emerging Order: God in an Age of Scarcity.* New York: G. P. Putnam's Sons, 1979.

———. *Entropy: A New World View.* New York: Viking Press, 1980.

————. *Biosphere Politics.* San Francisco: Harper San Francisco, 1991.

————, and Carol Grunewald. "The Greening of Economics." *Sojourners,* May 1992, pp. 6–8.

Robb, Carol S. and Carl J. Casebolt, eds. *Covenant for a New Creation: Ethics, Religion, and Public Policy.* Maryknoll, N.Y.: Orbis Books, 1991.

Robbins, J. K. "The Environment and Thinking about God." *Encounter,* Autumn 1987, pp. 401–15.

Rockefeller, Steven C. and John C. Elder. *Spirit and Nature: Why the Environment Is a Religious Issue.* Boston: Beacon Press, 1992.

Rolston, Holmes III. *Philosophy Gone Wild: Essays in Environmental Ethics.* Buffalo, N.Y.: Prometheus Press, 1986.

————. *Environmental Ethics: Duties to and Values in the Natural World.* Philadelphia: Temple University Press, 1988.

————. "Respect for Life: Christians, Creation, and Environmental Ethics." *CTNS Bulletin,* Spring 1991, pp. 1–8.

Ruether, Rosemary Radford. "Mother Earth and the Megamachine." Chap. 8 in *Liberation Theology: Human Hope Confronts Christian History and American Power.* New York: Paulist Press, 1972.

————. "Rich Nations/Poor Nations and the Exploitation of the Earth." *Dialog,* Summer 1974, pp. 201–07.

————. "New Woman and New Earth." Chap. 8 in *New Woman/New Earth: Sexist Ideologies and Human Liberation.* New York: Seabury Press, 1975.

————. "The Biblical Vision of the Ecological Crisis." *Christian Century,* 22 November 1978, pp. 1129–32.

————. "Ecology and Human Liberation: A Conflict between the Theology of History and the Theology of Nature?" Chap. 5 in *To Change the World: Christology and Cultural Criticism.* New York: Crossroad, 1981.

————. *Sexism and God-Talk: Toward a Feminist Theology.* Boston: Beacon Press, 1983.

————. "Facing up to Global Repentance." *Christianity and Crisis,* 19 August 1991, pp. 244–46.

————. *Gaia and God: An Ecofeminist Theology of Earth Healing.* San Francisco: Harper Collins, 1992.

Rust, Eric C. *Nature: Garden or Desert?* Waco, Tex.: Word Books, 1971.

Sabahire, M. "Saving the Earth to Save Life: an African Point of View." *Pro Mundi Vita Studies,* February 1990, pp. 19–26.

Samsonov, I. J. "Modern Ecological Crisis in the Light of the Bible and Christian World View." *Journal of the Moscow Patriarchate,* 1988, no. 11, pp. 40–45.

Santmire, H. Paul. "I–Thou, I–It, and I–Ens." *Journal of Religion,* July 1968, pp. 260–73.

————. "New Theology of Nature." *Lutheran Quarterly,* August 1968, pp. 290–308.

————. *Brother Earth: Nature, God and Ecology in Time of Crisis.* New York: Thomas Nelson, 1970.

————. "The Struggle for an Ecological Theology: A Case in Point." *Christian Century,* 4 March 1970, pp. 275–77.

————. "Reflections on the Alleged Ecological Bankruptcy of Western Theology." *Anglican Theological Review,* April 1975, pp. 131–52.

————. "Ecology, Justice and Theology: Beyond the Preliminary Skirmishes." *Christian Century,* 12 May 1976, pp. 460–64.

————. "The Liberation of Nature: Lynn White's Challenge Anew." *Christian Century,* 22 May 1985, pp. 530–33.

————. *The Travail of Nature: The Ambiguous Ecological Promise of Christian Theology.* Philadelphia: Fortress Press, 1985.

Schaeffer, Francis A. *Pollution and the Death of Man: The Christian View of Ecology.* Wheaton, Ill.: Tyndale House Publishers, 1970.

Scherer, Donald, ed. *Earth Ethics for Today and Tomorrow: Responsible Environmental Trade-Offs.* Bowling Green, Ohio: Bowling Green State University Environmental Center, 1974.

Schicker, G. E. "'An Institute for Earth Keeping.'" *Christian Century,* 14–21 September 1988, pp. 808–12.

Schillebeeck, Edward. "'All is Grace.' Creation and Grace in the Old and New Testaments." *Christ: The Experience of Jesus as Lord,* trans. John Bowden. New York: Seabury Press, 1980, pp. 515–30.

———. "Kingdom of God: Creation and Salvation." *Interim Report on the Books Jesus and Christ.* New York: Seabury Press, 1981, pp. 105–24.

Schmemann, Alexander. *For the Life of the World.* New York: National Student Christian Federation, 1963.

Schwartz, Hans. "Eschatological Dimensions of Ecology." *Zygon,* December 1974, pp. 323–38.

Scoby, D. R., ed. *Environmental Ethics: Studies of Man's Self Destruction.* Minneapolis: Burgess Publishing Co., 1971.

Scovell, Carl. "The Christian Creation." *Unitarian Universalist Christian,* Spring–Summer 1993, pp. 28–73.

Sharpe, Kevin J. and John M. Ker, eds. *Religion and Nature—with Charles Birch and Others.* Auckland: University of Auckland Chaplaincy Publication Trust, 1984.

Shaw, D. W. "Process Thought and Creation." *Theology,* July 1975, pp. 346–55.

Sheaffer, J. R. and R. H. Brand. *Whatever Happened to Eden?* Wheaton, Ill.: Tyndale House Publishers, 1980.

Sheldon, Joseph K. *Rediscovery of Creation: A Bibliographical Study of the Church's Response to the Environmental Crisis.* Metuchen, N.Y.: American Theological Library Association, Scarecrow Press, 1992.

———. "Creation Rediscovered." *World Christian,* vol. 9, no. 4, 1990, pp. 10–19.

Sherrell, Richard E., ed. *Ecology: Crisis and New Vision.* Richmond, Va.: John Knox Press, 1971.

Sherwood, Diane E. and Kristin Franklin. "Ecology and the Church: Theology and Action." *Christian Century,* 13 May 1987, pp. 472–74.

Shinn, Roger L. "Population and the Dignity of Man." *Christian Century,* 15 April 1970, pp. 442–48.

———. "Our Technological Time of Troubles." *Religion in Life,* Winter 1972, pp. 450–61.

———. "How Control Technology?" *Christianity and Crisis,* 29 October 1979, pp. 191–98.

———. "WCC Conference on Faith, Science and the Future." *Journal of Ecumenical Studies,* Winter 1980, pp. 206–07.

———, and Paul Abrecht, eds. *Faith and Science in an Unjust World: Report of the World Council of Churches' Conference on Faith, Science and the Future; Massachusetts Institute of Technology, Cambridge U.S.A., 12–24 July 1979.* 2 vols. Geneva: World Council of Churches, 1980.

———. *Forced Options: Social Decisions for the Twenty-First Century.* San Francisco: Harper and Row, 1982. (3d ed., published by Pilgrim Press, includes "Reconsiderations.")

Shoemaker, Dennis E. "Loving People, Loving Earth." *Christianity and Crisis,* 3 August 1987, pp. 260–63.

Sider, Ronald J. "Justice, Peace, and the Integrity of Creation." *World Christian,* vol. 9, no. 5, 1990, pp. 27–30.

———. *Rich Christians in an Age of Hunger.* Downers Grove: Ill.: InterVarsity Press, 1990.

———. "Redeeming the Environmentalists." *Christianity Today,* 21 June 1993, pp. 465–77.

Simon, Arthur. *Bread for the World.* New York/Ramsey, N.J.: Paulist Press and Grand Rapids, Mich.: Wm. B. Eerdmans, 1975. (Rev. ed., 1984.)

Sims, B. J. "The North American Conference on Religion and Ecology, Washington, DC, 16–18 May 1990: A Report to the Presiding Bishop." *Anglican and Episcopal History,* December 1990, pp. 441–52.

Sittler, Joseph. "A Theology of the Earth." *Christian Scholar,* September 1954, pp. 367–74.

———. "Called to Unity." *Ecumenical Review,* January 1962, pp. 177–87.

———. *The Care of the Earth and Other University Sermons.* Philadelphia: Fortress Press, 1964.

————. "Ecological Commitment as Theological Responsibility." *Zygon,* June 1970, pp. 172–81.

————. *The Ecology of Faith.* Philadelphia: Fortress Press, 1970.

————. *Essays on Nature and Grace.* Philadelphia: Fortress Press, 1972.

————. *Grace Notes and Other Fragments.* Philadelphia: Fortress Press, 1981.

Skolimowski, Henryk. *Eco-Theology: Toward a Religion for Our Times.* Madras: Vasawata Press, 1985.

Slattery, P. *Caretakers of Creation: Farmers Reflect on Their Life and Work.* Minneapolis: Augsburg, 1991.

Slusser, Dorothy M. and Gerald H. Slusser. *Technology: The God that Failed: The Environmental Catastophe.* Philadelphia: Westminster Press, 1971.

Smith, Harmon L. "Religious and Moral Aspects of Population Control." *Religion in Life,* Summer 1970, pp. 193–204.

Sobosan, Jeffrey G. *Bless the Beasts: A Spirituality of Animal Care.* New York: Crossroad, 1991.

Soelle, Dorothee with Shirley A. Cloyes. *To Work and To Love: A Theology of Creation.* Philadelphia: Fortress Press, 1984.

Soleri, Paolo. *The Omega Seed: An Eschatological Hypothesis.* Garden City, N.Y.: Anchor Books, Doubleday, 1981.

Sorrell, Roger. *St. Francis of Assissi: Tradition and Innovation in Western Christian Attitudes Toward the Environment.* New York: Oxford University Press, 1988.

Spring, David and Eileen Spring, eds. *Ecology and Religion in History.* New York: Harper and Row, 1974.

Squiers, Edwin R., ed. *The Environmental Crisis: The Ethical Dilemma.* Mancelona, Mich.: AuSable Trails Institute of Environmental Studies, 1982.

St. John, Donald. "Ecological Prayer: Toward an Ecological Spirituality." *Encounter,* Autumn 1982, pp. 337–48.

Stacey, W. David. "Christian View of Nature." *Expository Times,* September 1956, pp. 364–67.

Stafford, Tim. "Animal Lib." *Christianity Today,* 18 January 1990, pp. 19–23.

Stanovsky, Clinton. "Scientists and Theologians at MIT: A World Divided." *Christian Century,* 29 August–5 September 1979, pp. 814–15.

Stanton, Mark and Dennis B. Guernsey. "Christians' Ecological Responsibility: A Theological Introduction and Challenge." *Perspectives of Science and Christian Faith,* March 1993, pp. 2–7.

Steck, Odil Hannes. *World and Environment.* Nashville: Abingdon Press, 1978.

Steffen, Lloyd H. "In Defense of Dominion." *Environmental Ethics,* Spring 1992, pp. 63–80.

Steffenson, Dave, Robert S. Cook, and Walter J. Herrscher, eds. *Ethics for Environment: Three Religious Strategies.* Green Bay: University of Wisconsin-Green Bay, Ecumenical Center, 1973.

Stefferud, Alfred, ed. *Christians and the Good Earth.* New York: Friendship Press, 1972.

Stevenson, W. T. "Historical Consciousness and Ecological Crisis: A Theological Perspective." *Anglican Theological Review Supplementary Series,* November 1976, pp. 99–111.

Steward, R. G. *Environmental Stewardship.* Downers Grove, Ill.: InterVarsity Press, 1990.

Stewart, Charles. *Nature in Grace: A Study in the Theology of Nature.* Macon, Ga.: Mercer University Press, 1983.

Stivers, Robert L. *The Sustainable Society: Ethics and Economic Growth.* Philadelphia: Westminster Press, 1976.

————. "The Sustainable Society: Religious and Social Implications." *Review of Religious Research,* Fall 1979, pp. 71–86.

————. *Hunger, Technology, and Limits to Growth: Christian Responsibilities for Three Ethical Issues.* Minneapolis: Augsburg, 1984.

Stone, Glenn C., ed. *A New Ethic for a New Earth.* New York: Friendship Press, 1971.

Stone, R. H. "Ethics and Growth." *South East Asia Journal of Theology,* Spring 1972, pp. 40–62.

Stott, John R. W. and Robert T. Coote, eds. *Down to Earth: Studies in Christianity and Culture.*

Grand Rapids, Mich.: Wm. B. Eerdmans, 1980.

———. "Our Human Environment." Chap. 6 in *Involvement: Being a Responsible Christian in a Non-Christian Society.* Old Tappan, N.J.: Fleming H. Revell Company, 1984.

Streiffert, Kristi G. "The Earth Groans and Christians are Listening." *Christianity Today,* 2 September 1989, pp. 38–41.

Stuhlmacher, P. "The Ecological Crisis as a Challenge for Biblical Theology," trans. J. M. Stott. *Ex Auditu: an Annual of the Frederick Neumann Symposium on Theological Interpretation of Scripture,* 1987, pp. 1–15.

Swimme, Brian and Thomas Berry. *The Universe Story: From the Primordial Flaring Forth to the Ecozoic Era.* San Francisco: HarperCollins, 1992.

Taskforce on the Churches and Corporate Responsibility. *Model Code of Environmental Practice for Forest Land Management.* Toronto: TCCR, 1989.

Teilhard de Chardin. *The Phenomenon of Man,* trans. Bernard Wall. New York: Harper and Row, 1965.

———. *The Hymn of the Universe,* trans. Simon Bartholomew. New York: Harper and Row, 1965.

Therukattil, George. "Ecological Crisis—A Moral Dilemma." *Moral Theology Today,* ed. Bosco Puthur. Alwaye: Pontifical Institute, 1991, pp. 127–47.

Thompson, Frank and David Pollock. *The Iceberg and the Fire of Love: A Call to Ecological and Social Compassion.* Toronto: Anglican Book Centre, 1992.

Thompson, W. M. "'Dappled and Deep Down Things': A Meditation on Christian Ecological Trends." *Horizons,* Spring 1987, pp. 64–81.

Thorpe, W. H., E. Barker, Canon Dillistone, and Canon Edward Carpenter. "Nature." *Modern Churchman,* October 1970, pp. 9–42.

Thurber, L. N. "Care for the Creation as Mission Responsibility." *International Review of Mission,* April 1990, pp. 143–49.

Todrank, Gustave H. *The Eden Connection: A Study in Cultural Euthenics.* Lanham, Md.: University Press of America, 1981.

Tomkinson, E. W. F. "Ecological Reflection." *Heythrop Journal,* April 1985, pp. 187–96.

Trible, Phyllis. "Ancient Priests and Modern Polluters." *Andover Newton Quarterly,* December 1971, pp. 74–79.

Tubbs, James B., Jr. "Humble Dominion." *Theology Today,* January 1994, pp. 543–56.

Tucker, Mary Evelyn and John A. Grim. *World Views and Ecology.* Lewisburg, Pa.: Bucknell University Press, 1993.

Turnipseed, Lonnie. "US Conference for WCC Plenary." *Mid-Stream,* January 1977, pp. 142–44.

Underwood, Richard. "Ecological and Psychedelic Approaches to Theology." *Soundings,* Winter 1969, pp. 365–93.

Van Dyke, Fred. "Ecology and the Christian Mind." *Perspectives on Science and Christian Faith,* Summer 1991, pp. 266–82.

Van Hoeven, J. W., ed. *Justice, Peace and the Integrity of Creation.* Geneva: World Alliance of Reformed Churches, 1989.

Van Leeuwen, Raymond C. "Enjoying Creation—Within Limits." *Christianity Today,* 12 May 1989, pp. 34–37.

Vischer, Lukas, ed. *Rights of Future Generations, Rights of Nature.* Geneva: World Council of Churches, 1990.

Von Rohr Sauer, Alfred. "Ecological Notes from the Old Testament." *A Light unto My Path: Old Testament Studies in Honor of Jacob M. Myers,* ed. Howard N. Bream, Ralph D. Heim, and Carey A. Moore. Philadelphia: Temple University Press, 1974.

Vorster, W. S., ed. *Are We Killing God's Earth?* Pretoria: University of South Africa, 1987.

Waal, Victor de. "Towards a New Sacramental Theology." *Sobornost,* Winter 1974, pp. 697–707.

Wallace-Hadrill, David S. *The Greek Patristic View of Nature.* New York: Barnes Press, 1988.

Wang, B. C. "Demographic Theories and Policy Postitions on Population and Food." *Christian Scholar's Review,* vol. 9, no. 3, 1980, pp. 241–55.

Ward, B. *A New Creation? Reflections on the Environmental Issue.* Vatican City: Pontifical Commission on Justice and Peace, 1973.

Weiskel, Timothy C. "In Dust and Ashes: The Environmental Crisis in Religious Perspective." *Harvard Divinity Bulletin,* vol. 21, no. 3, 1992, pp. 11, 19, 23.

————, and Harvey G. Cox. *The Secular City and the Sacred Earth. Harvard Divinity Bulletin Supplement.* 1992.

Welbourn, F. B. "Man's Dominion." *Theology,* November 1975, pp. 561–68.

West, Charles C. "Justice within the Limits of the Created World." *Ecumenical Review,* January 1975, pp. 57–64.

————. "God—Woman/Man—Creation: Comments on the Ethics of the Relationship." *Ecumenical Review,* January 1981, pp. 13–28.

Westermann, Claus. "Creation and History in the Old Testament." *The Gospel and Human Destiny,* ed. Vilmos Vajta. Minneapolis: Augsburg, 1971, pp. 11–38.

————. *Creation,* trans. John J. Scullion. Philadelphia: Fortress Press, 1971.

————. *Blessing in the Bible and the Life of the Church,* trans. Keith Crim. Philadelphia: Fortress Press, 1978.

White, Lynn Jr. "The Historical Roots of Our Ecological Crisis." *Science,* 10 March 1967, pp. 1203–07.

————. "The Future of Compassion." *Ecumenical Review,* April 1978, pp. 99–109.

Whitehouse, W.A. "Towards a Theology of Nature." *Scottish Journal of Theology,* June 1964, pp. 129–45.

Whitney, Elspeth. "Ecotheology and History." *Environmental Ethics,* Summer 1993, pp. 151–69.

Wilkinson, Loren. "Christian Ecology of Death: Biblical Imagery and the Ecologic Crisis." *Christian Scholar's Review,* vol. 4, 1975, pp. 319–38.

————, ed. *Earthkeeping: Christian Stewardship of Natural Resources.* Grand Rapids, Mich.: Wm. B. Eerdmans, 1980 (revised and republished in 1991 as *Earthkeeping in the '90s: Stewardship of Creation).*

————. "Global Housekeeping: Lords or Servants." *Christianity Today,* 27 June 1980, pp. 752–56.

————. "Cosmic Christology and the Christian's Role in Creation." *Christian Scholar's Review,* vol. 11, no. 1, 1981, pp. 18–41.

————. "How Christian is the Green Agenda?" *Christianity Today,* 11 January 1993, pp. 16–20.

————. "Christianity and the Environment: Reflections on Rio and AuSable." *Science and Christian Belief,* October 1993, pp. 139–45.

Williams, George H. *Wilderness and Paradise in Christian Thought: The Biblical Experience of the Desert in the History of Christianity and the Paradise Theme in the Theological Idea of the University.* New York: Harper and Brothers, 1962.

————. "Christian Attitudes Toward Nature." *Christian Scholar's Review,* Fall 1971, pp. 3–35.

Wink, Walter. "The 'Elements of the Universe' in Biblical and Scientific Perspective." *Zygon,* September 1978, pp. 225–48.

————. "Ecobible: the Bible and Ecojustice." *Theology Today,* January 1993, pp. 465–77.

Winter, Gibson. *Liberating Creation: Foundations of Religious Social Ethics.* New York: Crossroad, 1981.

World Council of Churches. "Global Environment, Responsible Choice, and Social Justice." *Ecumenical Review,* October 1971, pp. 438–42.

————. *Now is the Time.* Geneva: World Council of Churches, 1990.

World Evangelical Fellowship. "'Evangelical Christianity and the Environment': Summarizing Committee Report." *Transformation,* 1992, pp. 27–30.

Wright, C. J. H. *God's People in God's Land: Family, Land, and Property in the Old Testament.* Grand Rapids, Mich.: Wm. B. Eerdmans, 1990.

Wright, Nancy G. and Donald G. Kill. *Ecological Healing: A Christian View.* Maryknoll, N.Y.: Orbis Press, 1993.

Wright, R. T. *Biology through the Eyes of Faith.* San Francisco: Harper and Row, 1989.

Yancey, Philip. "A Voice Crying in the Rainforest." *Christianity Today,* 22 July 1991, pp. 26–28.
Yasuda, Haruo. "Environmental Issues." *Christianity in Japan, 1971–1990,* ed. Yoshinobu Kumazawa and David L. Swimme. Tokyo: Kyo Bun Kwan, 1991, pp. 114–29.
Young, R. V., Jr. "A Conservative View of Environmental Affairs." *Environmental Ethics,* Fall 1979, pp. 241–54.
Zizioulas, John D. "Preserving God's Creation: Three Lectures on Theology and Ecology." *King's Theological Review,* Spring 1989, pp. 1–5; Autumn 1989, pp. 41–45; Spring 1990, pp. 1–5.
———. *Creation as Eucharist: A Theological Approach to the Ecological Problem.* 1992.

There are a number of small magazines and journals which contain considerable material related to this bibliography. Instead of listing these essays, I ask the reader to consult the journals as a whole.

Anthropos: Justice, Ecology, Spirit, Community, Box 178, Torrance, CA 90505.
Anticipation is published by the World Council of Churches. Especially during the period before and after the MIT Conference on Faith, Science and the Future, it included many relevant articles.
Christian Social Action (formerly *Engage-Social Action*) is published by the Board of Church and Society, United Methodist Church, 100 Maryland Ave. NE, Washington, DC 20002.
Daughters of Sarah. Chicago: Daughters of Sarah, Inc.
Earth Matters: A Journal of Faith Community and Resources. Published by the National Catholic Rural Life Conference, 4625 Beaver Ave., Des Moines IA, 50310-2199.
Earthkeeping: A Quarterly of Faith and Agriculture is published by Christian Farmers Federation of Ontario, 115 Woolwich St. Guelph, Ont., Canada.
Earthlight: Magazine of Spirituality and Ecology is published by the Pacific Yearly Meeting Committee on Unity with Nature. 1558 Mercy St., Mountain View, CA 94041.
Eco-Justice Quarterly (formerly, *The Egg: An Eco-Justice Quarterly*) is published by the Eco-Justice Project and Network, Anabel Taylor Hall, Cornell University, Ithaca, NY 14853-1001.
Epiphany: A Journal of Faith and Insight is published by Epiphany for Christ the Saviour Brotherhood, South Portland, ME.
ESA Advocate is published by Evangelicals for Social Action, 5107 Newhall St., Philadelphia, PA 19144.
Firmament: The Quarterly of Christian Ecology is published by The North American Conference on Christianity and Ecology.
Journal of the American Scientific Affiliation is published by the American Scientific Affiliation, 5 Douglas Ave., Elgin IL 60120.
Teilhard Perspective (formerly *Teilhard Studies*) is published by the American Teilhard Association, 40 Hillside Lane, Syosset, NY 11791.

In addition, many journals have had special issues on the topic.

American Journal of Theology and Philosophy. "Technology, Culture and Environment." January 1983.
ARC: The Journal of the Faculty of Religious Studies, McGill University. "Religious Attitudes toward Nature." Spring 1990.
CBRF Journal. "Earth Matters: Stewardship and Dominion in God's Garden." March 1991.
Christian Century. "The Environmental Crisis." 7 October 1970.
Christianity and Crisis. "God's Earth and Our Own." 14 May 1990.
CTNS Bulletin: The Center for Theology and the Natural Sciences. "The Church and the Environmental Crisis." Summer 1990.
Dialog. "Creation and Redemption." Fall 1964. "Man and His Environment." Summer 1970.
Direction. "Earthkeeping." Fall 1992.

Ecumenical Review. "Faith, Science and the Future." October 1979. "Come Holy Spirit, Renew Thy Whole Creation." April 1990.

Eternity. "What Are We Doing to God's Earth?" 1970.

Evangelical Review of Theology. "Evangelicals and the Environment: Theological Foundations for Christian Environmental Stewardship." April 1993.

Event. "Man and His Environment." 1970.

Foundations. "Ecology and Justice." April–June 1974.

IDOC-North America. "A Theology of Survival." 12 September 1970. "Alternatives to Catastrophe." October 1972.

International Review of Mission. "The Holy Spirit, Mission and Renewal of the Earth." April 1990.

Lutheran Quarterly. "Reflections on Theological Symbols: Man and Nature." November 1971.

Missionalia. "Mission and Ecology." April 1991.

Modern Churchman. "Nature, Man and God." vol. 14, no. 1, 1970."The State of the Ark." vol. 32, no. 2, 1990.

Pro Mundi Vita Studies. "Christians and the Ecological Consciousness." February 1990.

Process Studies. "Ecology." Summer 1993.

Reformed Review. "Society, City, and Ecology: A Theological Encounter." Spring 1972.

Religion and Intellectual Life. "Repurposing Education: The American College in the Ecological Age." Winter 1989.

Religious Education. "Ecology and Religious Education." January–February 1971.

―――. "Religious Education and the Integrity of Creation." Winter 1990.

Review and Expositor. "Ecology and the Church." Winter 1972.

Sojourners. "The Cry of Creation." March 1990.

Theology Digest. "Creation and Technology." Fall 1979.

Word and World. "Cosmos and Creation." Fall 1984. "The Land." Winter 1986. "Creation in Crisis." Spring 1991.

Zygon. "Conference on Ethics and Ecology of the Institute on Religion in the Age of Science." December 1970. "Papers from the Meeting of the Science and Religion Forum on Man's Responsibility for Nature." September 1977.